Unbelievable Crimes Volume Seven

Unbelievable Crimes, Volume 7

Daniela Airlie

Published by Daniela Airlie, 2023.

While every precaution has been taken in the preparation of this book, the publisher assumes no responsibility for errors or omissions, or for damages resulting from the use of the information contained herein.

UNBELIEVABLE CRIMES VOLUME SEVEN

First edition. November 13, 2023.

Copyright © 2023 Daniela Airlie.

Written by Daniela Airlie.

Table of Contents

Unbelievable Crimes Volume Seven: Macabre Yet Unknown True Crime Stories.. 1

Introduction.. 3

Surviving The Unsurvivable.. 5

Party At My House.. 19

Prejudice And Injustice... 31

Evil Desires.. 41

Beyond Recognition 53

Twisted Revenge 63

Dungeon Beneath The Cellar....................................... 73

Murder, He Wrote 83

A Six-Figure Murder... 91

Final Thoughts..103

The right of Daniela Airlie as the publisher and owner of this work has been asserted in accordance with the Copyright, Designs, and Patents Act 1988. No part of this publication may be reproduced in any format without the publisher's prior written consent. This book is for entertainment and informational purposes only.

Although research from various sources has gone into this book, neither the author nor publisher will be held responsible for any inaccuracies. To the best of the knowledge of the author, all information within this publication is factually correct and derived from researching these cases thoroughly. The author may offer speculation and/or opinion about the topics covered throughout this book.

Danielaairlie.carrd.co[1]

---

1. http://danielaairlie.carrd.co

Introduction

Welcome to *Unbelievable Crimes Volume Seven.*

This volume takes us all over the globe: Ireland, Melbourne, Florida, and Scotland, to name a few. Each one is as shocking as the next, with tales so unsettling it's hard to believe they're true.

As many of you already know, the series' premise is to document lesser-known crimes: the tales that didn't get the same press coverage as, say, Ted Bundy, but where the story is equally as alarming. This is for two reasons. One to ensure the perpetrator of these crimes is remembered for their vile acts. And two, more importantly, to try and make sure the victim's story gets told and isn't forgotten.

In this anthology, I cover the case of a woman whose violent husband escalated his violence to unimaginable heights. I recount the tale of a teenager who harbors the desire to kill his parents - and goes through with his murderous impulses in a violent manner. Then there's the case of a serial sex offender who, frustratingly, kept getting released from prison for his perverted crimes - only to re-offend. I also tell the tale of a young couple who were brutally beaten for nothing other than the style of clothing they wore.

You'll learn about these crimes and five more cases in this seventh installment of the series. And, as I always have to mention, please know that this book details violent crimes, sexual abuse, and real-life suffering - bear this in mind if you feel these subjects are too heavy. With that said, let's begin.

Surviving The Unsurvivable

In the USA, three women are killed by their spouses each day. To put that in sobering perspective, between now and this time tomorrow, three females will die a violent death at the hands of their abusive partner. That's just in the US; in 2020, almost 50,000 females worldwide were murdered by their intimate partner, ex, or jilted love interest. *That's 137 women killed per day.*

These truly horrific stats become all the more sinister the more you think about them. What about all of the instances of domestic abuse that led up to each murderous climax? If 50,000 women lose their lives to a partner each year, how many millions are enduring violence every day? Disturbingly, almost 36% of women in the US have experienced rape, violence, and/or stalking from a spouse in their lifetime.

Teri Jendusa-Nicolai is a name among those depressing stats. She endured abuse at the hands of her controlling husband for years, and her separation from him led to unthinkable violence at the hands of the man who proclaimed to love her. David Larsen was willing to strip his two daughters of their mother and end a woman's life - all because he couldn't deal with his former lover moving on from him.

On January 31, 2004, Sheriff Christopher Schmaling was on duty on a freezing evening in Racine, Wisconsin. Although Racine wasn't exactly crime-free (most of the illegal activity was petty), Schmaling hadn't been expecting to be working on a missing persons case. It wasn't a typical missing person's case either: the police had already pinpointed their primary suspect in Teri Jendusa-Nicolai's disappearance. They just needed to make sure the victim was found alive, but time was ticking.

Teri had been her husband's verbal, emotional, and physical punchbag for years. She feared his harsh insults, cutting put-downs, and scolding criticism. If so much as a towel was folded incorrectly, David Larsen would be sure to yell and scream at his wife for her supposed infraction. In fact, the man had his wife in such a state of fear and panic all the time she'd hide any evidence of smashed plates or glasses. Instead of being able to tell her husband that she'd accidentally dropped the kitchenware, she would scoop up the mess and hide it in her neighbor's bin. She'd then buy another glass or plate to disguise that one was missing.

David's fierce temper and military-like rule over Teri encroached on every aspect of the abused woman's life. She couldn't even shower in peace - David insisted the bathroom door was always left open. Privacy was disallowed. Teri's autonomy was stripped away.

Food was often the catalyst for David flying into a rage. How Teri prepared dinner and cooked their meals was something the abusive man would use to berate and criticize his wife. If something wasn't prepared how David liked, he'd scold his wife for "wasting his money." It seemed no matter what Teri did, she could never do it to her husband's satisfaction.

Where mealtimes would often be the source of David's ranting and raving, it eventually became Teri's breaking point. In one particularly ugly argument over spaghetti, Teri felt such fear of her husband's rage she fled to the basement and hid. All because she'd let the ingredients sit on the kitchen countertop too long. According to David, anyway, who was incensed by this.

Here she was, a 30-year-old mother of two, hiding in a box in her marital home because she was afraid of her husband; this upsetting realization hit Teri as she cowered in the basement. It was at this moment Teri decided enough was enough. She couldn't take it anymore.

This incident - similar to so many she'd endured before - also made Teri come to understand that her violent husband may soon turn his sadistic attention to their children. Her young daughters were growing up fast, and there was no way Teri was going to allow David to treat the girls with the same wicked cruelty he subjected her to. Her mind was made up - she was getting out. Even if it meant struggling for a short while and having to deal with David in court, she was going to face these fears for the good of her children.

Teri packed up some essentials and took herself and her daughters to a shelter. She filed for divorce. While she was far from where she wanted to be in life, Teri felt safe in the knowledge that she'd saved not only herself but her children from years of torment and bullying.

The day Teri and David's divorce was finalized, the pair had to meet in court. As expected, David was in floods of tears, but Teri knew they weren't tears for the broken marriage - they were tears of anger. David had lost the grip of control and power he once had over Teri. Any pangs of sympathy she had for David were soon dampened when the sobbing man said to his ex-wife, "You're going to regret this."

At the time, this was seen as a bitter comment. In hindsight, it was a sinister promise from David.

The years passed by, and Teri managed to get back on her feet. She even met a new partner, Nick Nicolai, whom she married. Nick was a doting and attentive stepfather to Teri's children, and there was no fear of violence or abuse in this marriage. Life was good for the blended family.

But David wasn't going to make things so easy for his ex. The man was still angry and bitter toward Teri three years after their divorce. He fought her for custody of their girls, still wanting to retain a significant element of control over his former spouse. Their children were the only way he could do this.

Ultimately, the court awarded David joint custody of their girls, something that Teri had wanted to avoid. She was uneasy about David being left alone with their children. After all, he didn't think twice about hurting Teri. Now, the only way David could get to her was via their daughters. The whole situation left Teri feeling disheartened but left her no choice but to allow David unsupervised visitation.

It was up to Teri to drop the girls off at David's as well as pick them up. As you can imagine, David didn't make these interactions anything but stressful for Teri. He'd verbally abuse her and sometimes lash out physically, too. As a result, Teri began refusing to attend David's home, instead only dropping the girls off in a busy public place. Outside fast food places or busy parking lots were Teri's preferred meeting point, and for good reason. Like most cowardly abusers, David wouldn't dare lash out in front of others.

Around this time, Teri had successfully got a restraining order against her ex. While this went some way in protecting Teri - the order meant David had to get rid of his firearms - it also posed to be problematic. The pair shared children, and Teri couldn't always rely on others to drop them off and pick them up from their father's home. So, despite the restraining order, Teri found herself back to taxiing her daughters to and from David's home.

David had apparently moved on and was dating another woman. This didn't stop him from obsessing over his failed marriage and his former wife, though. David remained in the house he and Teri had once called their marital home. He kept videotapes of their wedding and would play them for his four and six-year-olds. He kept Teri's wedding dress and photo albums of the pair. During one showing of their wedding video, David told his daughters the recording was proof that their mother "didn't keep her promises." Perhaps David didn't grasp the irony of his comment since, in his wedding vows, he promised to love and cherish Teri. In reality, he abused and controlled her.

In late January 2004, David asked Teri to come collect Amanda and Holly from him. Teri felt uneasy about the collection - she never knew what to expect from her explosive ex - but was hopeful her former husband was slowly moving on. Teri hadn't forgotten that precisely three years ago to the day she'd finalized her divorce from David, and she doubted he'd forgotten either. Still, he'd found a new partner, and Teri hoped this would be the catalyst for him moving on for good.

Teri pulled up on David's snowy driveway, knocked on the door, and was greeted by something she didn't expect: a calm, cheerful David. "The girls are playing hide and seek," he told Teri, explaining that Amanda and Holly wanted their mother to find them. Teri's instinct - and prior experience - told her not to enter the property. But, the thought of her children hiding in the house waiting for their mother to find them made her take that fateful step inside her former home. She didn't want to upset her babies or for them to think she didn't want to play with them.

However, Teri's gut instinct had been right. David had set a trap to lure his victim in, and she'd just been snared.

Nick Nicolai was sitting at home waiting for Teri to return with the girls. It shouldn't have taken her long to drive by and collect them. When his wife wasn't home within the hour, he was getting panicky. When two hours passed, he was pacing the living room, hoping her car would pull up any minute now. By the time three hours passed, Nick knew something was up. He called the police and let them know his wife was missing, and offered them David's address. Normally, a wife running some errands for three or more hours isn't cause for concern - we all lose track of time sometimes. For Nick, it was the fact Teri wasn't home after going to David's; he knew something sinister had happened.

With Nick giving the 911 dispatcher David's address, they were able to cross-reference that with a disturbing call they'd had earlier in the day. A woman had made an unnerving, wheezy call to the police, giving the exact same address. The call ended before the caller could offer more details, but the picture became clear: the panicked call was made by Teri, and her captor was more than likely David Larsen.

The police headed to David's address, but frustratingly, nobody was there. Officers did a thorough search of the place and were left with no other option than to knock on neighbors' doors to see if they knew anything. As it turned out, some neighbors had seen something interesting: David towing Teri's car.

This piece of information sealed David's fate as the number one suspect in his ex's vanishing. But there was another problem: the police couldn't find David. Not only that, they couldn't find Holly or Amanda. Things were not looking good. Nick had told officers just how nasty and bitter David had been over his ex leaving him, and the date - the third anniversary of their divorce - had possibly caused his rage to go into overdrive.

Every hour passing without a lead lowered the chance of Teri and her children being found alive.

As a manhunt was in the process of being formed, another frantic call to police came in. It was the same female caller from earlier, but this time, she managed to give her name: Teri Jendusa-Nicolai. She was alive, but the details she gave didn't look promising. She had been stuffed inside a bin and was being driven by her ex in his pickup truck.

The call ended.

What police didn't know was that Teri had been badly beaten - almost to the point of death. David had used a baseball bat to batter his ex to the point of immobility. He then coldly stuffed her body inside a bin, knowing she was dying, and took off to an unknown location. The fate of his daughters was still unknown.

Officers got a warrant for David's home and were met with a disturbing find. Teri's sweatpants were strewn on the floor, and blood stains soiled the carpet. Alarmingly, there was also a handgun case without the gun inside - it seemed David had taken it with him. He clearly hadn't disposed of his guns as the restraining order laid out, and officers were getting incredibly concerned about his children. *Could he have done the unthinkable to get back at Teri?*

For now, all they knew was Teri was in great danger, the prime suspect was likely armed, and they had to work fast to ensure Teri was found alive. Time passed at what felt like super-speed, and leads were not forthcoming. Volunteers headed out to nearby communities to knock on doors and check inside empty, yet-to-be-sold homes to see if David had left his victim there. Despite their hard work, they found nothing. An Amber Alert was issued, which also yielded no results. *Somebody, somewhere, must know something* - but it seemed that somebody was David Larsen, and he was nowhere to be found.

Officers only had one last hope: that David would turn up for work that evening. Sure enough, David showed up on time for his air traffic controller job and was met by the police. They played it gently with the man, avoided accusations, and simply asked for his help in finding his missing ex-wife. "Would you mind coming to the station?" officers asked, treating the man as if he were a helpful witness rather than suspect number one.

David really didn't have a choice - if he declined the invite to help find the missing mother of his children, he'd incriminate himself. So, he voluntarily went with officers, who sat him down for questioning.

Initially, David told them Teri hadn't shown up to collect the girls, so he'd dropped them off at his new partner's house before he began his shift. Officers were dispatched to David's girlfriend's home, where, thankfully, Holly and Amanda were found safe and sound. But where was Teri?

The girls told officers they'd not seen their mother. They had been staying with their dad, but at one point earlier that day, he'd locked them in his back bedroom. When he came to get them out, they were driven to his girlfriend's home instead of going home to their mother.

Things weren't looking good for Teri. By now, she'd been missing for almost a whole 24 hours. The phone calls to the police had been when she'd just been brutally attacked and was likely still full of adrenaline. If David had dumped her somewhere, the subzero temperature may have killed her by now. Maybe David had made use of the gun he'd taken from his home. The macabre possibilities were endless. None of them were promising.

After playing good cop with David for a while, with time quickly passing, they began to unravel his lies. They told him they'd found Teri's sweatpants in his home, pools of blood on his carpet, and knew that he had taken one of his guns from the house when he left. This left David scrambling for an explanation, but he eventually found one: that Teri had attacked him and he'd retaliated in self-defense. At this point, David began to get emotional. He hadn't been emotional during the interview until this point, but it seems the pressure of being caught out in his lies had gotten to him. He wasn't getting his own way, much like in the divorce court, where he sobbed over his wife leaving him. The tears weren't for anyone else but himself.

David couldn't tell officers what he'd done with Teri since it was a "blur." He recalled everything else clearly, but the aftermath of her attacking him suddenly left his memory. The man was arrested as a suspect in Teri's possible murder and, as a result, was stripped of his personal belongings. Among them was his wallet, where they found an address for a storage unit. It was a long shot, but officers called the number on the card and were surprised to know that not only had David visited the storage place that morning, but he was also renting a unit there.

Immediately, officers were dispatched to the location, readying themselves to find the remains of Teri Jendusa-Nicolai. The temperatures were well below freezing, and the amount of blood the victim had likely lost by now would be huge factors in her not surviving the past 24 hours. Officers opened David's unit, and in the corner of the freezing container was a bin. With bated breath, the police opened the container to find the freezing, heavily bloodied body of Teri. Her skull had been caved in. Her body was so broken that officers didn't dare move her from the bin for fear of killing her. She was less than an hour away from death; had officers been much later in getting to the storage unit, their discovery would have been that of a dead body.

While Teri was alive - just - heartbreakingly, the fetus inside her was no longer. The brutal and sadistic violence she'd endured at the hands of her ex had been enough to snuff out the life of her unborn baby.

Paramedics arrived on the scene and managed to get Teri to the safety of the hospital. It was touch and go for a while, and saving her life was paramount.

The location of David's storage unit became a sinister aspect of this case. His role as an air traffic controller put him in a tower, from which he had a perfect view of the storage unit he held Teri in. Could he have relished in the idea he could look over and see the place where his wife was slowly dying? Thankfully, he never got the chance. As soon as Teri was rushed to hospital, David was charged with attempted murder.

The thing that saved Teri's life, ultimately, was her cell phone (which David had neglected to take from her) and her will to live for her daughters. The beating she endured, prolonged and brutal, was enough to kill her. The subzero temperatures, in which she was held half-clothed, were enough to kill her. But Teri held on for as long as she could, drifting in and out of consciousness, all the while willing God to keep her alive for her daughters.

The following year, in August, David Larsen pleaded guilty to attempted first-degree intentional homicide. He was initially handed 35 years for his disturbing crime, but this was later increased to life in jail.

Recovery wasn't easy for Teri. The assault had left her unable to walk, her lack of toes proving to be another obstacle to overcome. In all, she underwent ten operations to fix her broken body from the sadism her ex had inflicted upon her. When she was eventually released from hospital care, her body and her mind weren't quite aligned. Teri wanted to play with her daughters and tuck them in at night. Her body wouldn't allow it; she couldn't even climb the stairs. It would take some time for her battered and bruised body to recover, but when it did, Teri was left with an ironic thought: the person who'd tried to end her existence in such an evil way had been dealt with his own existence being reduced to almost nothing.

Once, she was told what to do and when to do it, and she was chastised for her "wrongdoings." Now, she lives a life of freedom, happiness, and contentment. David now lives a life similar to the one he forced Teri to endure. He's told what he can and can't do, what he eats, what time he eats, and I don't imagine there's much privacy where he is.

Miraculously, Teri and Nick had a baby boy, making their little family complete.

Party At My House

Tyler Hadley's parents were out of town in Orlando, by some accounts. Tyler was left at the Port St. Lucie, Florida, home on his own, and the 17-year-old had been spreading the word that a party was happening at his house. He told his fellow Port St. Lucie High schoolmates, but nobody took the teen seriously - they didn't believe his mother and father would let him throw a huge party at their home.

However, Tyler was adamant he would be hosting a gathering that weekend, and on Saturday, July 16, 2011, he posted on his social media page: *party at my crib tonight.*

Still, some of his friends weren't convinced Tyler's parents wouldn't turn up and throw them out. *What if your parents come home*, one classmate replied. *They won't*, Tyler insisted. *Trust me.*

The teens didn't need to be told twice. Port St. Lucie wasn't exactly built for the younger person in mind. There was rarely, if ever, anything exciting going on for the teens who grew up in the city. In fact, it was catered to the older person, peppered with golf courses and bingo halls, which left the Port St. Lucie youth with little to do on evenings and weekends. With Tyler promising a big party at his home, word spread fast.

Tyler wasn't exactly popular at school. In fact, he was considered a relatively quiet kid who hung around with the stoners and troublemakers. The teen was tall, brooding, and mostly standoffish, and although most people recognized his face, very few people knew who Tyler was. Still, with little else to do on that humid Saturday night, the open invite was accepted by dozens of local kids, and by 11:30 that evening, the first group of partygoers had arrived and knocked on Hadley's front door.

The teen answered, his pupils as big as saucers from the ecstasy pills he'd taken hours earlier. Tyler invited the gaggle of teenagers inside but warned them, "I don't want no one smoking inside. It's my parent's house." Little did the guests know, Tyler's parents were still in the house - they were in the master bedroom, blood dried to their pale faces, hidden underneath random household items.

Blake and Mary Jo Hadley had moved to the affluent area of Port St. Lucie seven years before Tyler was born. Blake's parents had retired there, and the couple followed them to make sure they settled in okay. The Hadleys would end up staying in the safe, calm area, believing it would be the perfect place to raise a family. Blake worked as an engineer, and Mary Jo was a school teacher.

Tyler was seemingly close to his mother and father as he grew up. He would play basketball with his dad and playfight with him in the family's pool. His mother was a source of comfort and affection for the quiet boy.

While he notably kept to himself, Tyler was also known to act out during class occasionally. He wouldn't necessarily play class clown but rather do random, unpredictable things such as mooing like a cow as the teacher spoke. Sure, it would garner a laugh, but probably due to the weirdness of the situation, not because Tyler was doing something amusing. Sometimes, the boy would also burst out laughing for no apparent reason. Eccentric was how some of his classmates would later describe him. Some would call him bizarre. Nobody could read the teenager.

As the boy got older, the boredom of living in such a peaceful place seemed to cause him to rebel. Along with a group of other teens, he dragged a sofa to the River Park Wildlife Preserve with the intent of setting it on fire. When the gang caused the couch to burst into flames much higher than expected, they fled the scene. The fire department had to come and put the spreading flames out. Tyler was caught for the dangerous behavior, but all he got was a warning not to do it again.

Blake and Mary Jo Hadley couldn't reason with their son or quell his desire to engage in troublesome acts. In fact, it seemed Tyler was spiraling out of control, and the parents were helpless to stop him. The usually easy-going parents were finding they had to start getting strict with their boy, something they'd never had to be before. This didn't go down well with Tyler, who wasn't used to such restrictions.

In the months leading up to his big party, Tyler had been arrested for burglary and aggravated battery on separate occasions. To help correct the wayward boy, he was given two weeks of house arrest. In a bid to make sure Tyler knew his actions had consequences, Mary Jo confiscated her son's cell phone during this period. This did not go down well with the teenager who lived his life on social media.

Before having his phone taken away, Tyler made sure to delete any incriminating conversations on his device. Mainly, he got rid of messages to his drug dealers. *Don't text me about drugs*, he wrote in one text to a friend. In the same message, Tyler admitted he thought about killing himself sometimes and confided in his friend that all his smiles were fake. In an effort to cheer the teenager up, the friend offered to "smoke a bowl" with him.

Just one month before the fateful party at the Hadley house, Tyler had been out on a heady Friday night. He arrived home extremely drunk and, in his own words, was "smashed." The teen was stumbling about and acting in a way that disturbed his mother, who'd been awoken by her son's drunken behavior. Prior to making it home that night, Tyler had unzipped his pants and urinated all over a female friend's bed.

In a desperate bid to get her boy back on the right track, Mary Jo immediately got her son admitted to a mental health clinic. With Tyler being under 18, he had no choice in the matter. He had daily counseling, was given psychiatric treatment, and every effort was made to get to the root cause of Tyler's erratic and often violent behavior. Mary Jo insisted she never thought her son would hurt her, but she was fearful that he would do something irreversible to himself. She was half right; she had no idea her son also harbored desires to kill his parents from time to time.

There were some fears, though, that her son was depressed. Mary Jo herself had dealt with mental health struggles in the past, and she wondered if she'd somehow passed these struggles down to her son. Indeed, when Tyler was in his early teens, his mother took him to get human growth hormone injections. She feared her small, portly boy would be bullied and begin to despise himself. To avoid this scenario and her son having poor self-esteem, she thought injections were the way to go. Tyler would grow to be tall and skinny.

After the referral to the mental health clinic at Mary Jo's insistence, it seemed, to the mother at least, that Tyler was making improvements. Perhaps Mary Jo was just trying to will her son's good behavior into existence, but she had been telling people her boy was almost "back to himself." Little did she know, her son was experimenting with ecstasy, and his dark thoughts weren't subsiding - they were escalating.

In the weeks leading up to the murder of Blake and Mary Jo, Tyler had, in fact, told one of his friends he was plotting to kill his parents. The teenager also noted that having a huge party after slaying a mother and father had "never been done before" and admitted this was how he wanted to celebrate the killings. The friend didn't believe Tyler - after all, he was known to say strange things all the time.

Tyler posted on social media a fortnight later, "party at my crib tonight." Hours before this, he'd slain his parents.

Rewind to earlier that day, Tyler was consumed by thoughts of bloody murder. *Today was the day*, he thought. He covertly found both parents' cell phones and hid them. He also got the family dog, a friendly labrador, and locked him in the wardrobe. The rationale for this was to prevent the protective pet from stopping Tyler from carrying out the murders successfully.

The teen was nervous that he'd not be able to carry out the plan without the help of some false courage. He took three ecstasy tablets late that afternoon, and by the time they kicked in, he knew it was time.

Mary Jo was on her computer in the living area. Clutching a claw hammer, Tyler snuck up behind his mother as she typed and swung as hard as he could. He hit the woman with the sharp claw end. The injury wasn't enough to debilitate her, and she managed to turn round and see her son holding the bloodied weapon. "Why?" she pleaded. "Why not?" was the reply.

The teenager resumed his attack, smashing his mother in the skull multiple times as the woman shrieked for help. Blake heard his wife screaming and raced to the living area to be met with a gut-churning sight: his son, standing over his unrecognizable wife, blood pooling around her. In Tyler's hand was a crimson-colored hammer. In shock, Blake asked his son the same question as his wife: why? The response from Tyler was the same: why not?

The teenager then lunged toward his father, swinging the sharp claw end of the hammer into the man's skull. He cracked his father in the head multiple times, blood spattering all around, including on Tyler's face. It was a violent, feral attack that Blake and Mary Jo would not survive.

After the ferocious ambush, Tyler stood back to see the damage he'd done. His bloodied, lifeless parents lay before him. All he could think about was the party he was going to have that night. For that to happen, he needed to get cleaned up.

For the next few hours, the teen - still fueled by the effects of ecstasy - cleaned up the copious amounts of blood and fluid from the floors and walls. He then dragged his parents' bodies to the main bedroom and threw the cleaning products on top of them. He shut the door on them and sent out his party invite. Of course, any good party needs supplies, and Tyler took his parent's credit card to head out and collect cash from an ATM.

People began trickling in just after 11 pm that night, with some people joking as they entered that they could "smell dead bodies" in the house. If only they knew. Within an hour or so, 60 teens were at the Hadley house, although most of them would admit they'd never spoken to Tyler before - they were just there for the party.

The guests helped themselves to food in the cupboards, used the floor as a trash can and ashtray, made use of the drinks cabinet, smashed their used beer bottles on the driveway, and cranked the music up as loud as it would go. The desecration of the family home didn't concern Tyler. The noise bothered him - he needed the guests to quiet down before the neighbors called the police.

Just an hour into the party, the booze was running dry. Tyler pulled out a wad of 20s from his pocket and asked a 21-year-old to go into the gas station for some light beer. While the teens were awaiting more drinks arriving, Tyler told a girl that his father was dead. She thought Tyler meant his dad had died years ago, not mere hours earlier. Certainly, she couldn't know that it was at the hands of Tyler.

Partygoers were praising Tyler for his party, commending him for throwing the biggest party of the year. As they did, a drunken teen ran into the house, shirtless, holding next door's mailbox. This infuriated Tyler, who was doing his best to avoid the police being called. Sure enough, the mailbox was returned to its rightful place within minutes.

People were still arriving. They would wander the house in search of the bathroom and, in doing so, would wind up at the master bedroom. The door was locked. Beneath the door was a big, black stain - at least, it looked black. The lights were dim, but it looked like an oil spill or some dark liquid had pooled underneath the door. The teens shrugged and continued looking for the bathroom. They'd just been feet away from the corpses of Blake and Mary Jo Hadley.

The more kids arrived, the more they complained of a funny smell. By 1 am, the house was trashed. Food, drink, and cigarettes coated the kitchen tiles, broken glass filled the driveway, and drunken bodies filled the living area. By this point, still high, Tyler confessed to a friend, "I did some things." For whatever reason, it took Tyler this long to process the finality of what he'd done earlier in the day. "I'm freaking out," he told the drunken friend, who asked him why. "I killed somebody," Tyler said.

This didn't garner much of a response from the friend. "That's your business," the teenager replied before telling Tyler he didn't need to know any more about it.

Shortly after, Tyler went up to another friend and told him he was going to kill himself. When the concerned friend asked why, Tyler said he had to kill himself because he'd be going to jail for murder. This was Tyler talking, though - he always said weird things. Nobody took much notice. The teen then told his old friend Kim that he was going to jail for decades. When she asked why, he smiled that she'd know why the following day.

Finally, Tyler bumped into his childhood friend Mike. He blurted out, "I killed my parents." For the first time all night, someone took Tyler's confession seriously. Could Tyler be telling the truth? After all, both his parents' cars were still in the driveway. How could they be in Orlando if they didn't drive there?

Tyler led Mike to the master bedroom. He opened the door slowly, and inside the dark room was a heap of blood-soaked towels, cleaning products, and a pile of junk. Sticking out beneath the pile of rubbish was a human leg. Mike looked on in shock as Tyler recounted the murders to his friend.

Once Tyler had finished bludgeoning his parents to death, he wrapped bath towels around their collapsed skulls and dragged them to the bedroom. The couple lay face down next to one another.

Despite his shock at what he'd just seen, Mike didn't run from the Hadley house. In fact, he stayed for almost another hour and prior to leaving, took a selfie with his old friend Tyler. After all, he reasoned, he would likely never see him again.

By 2 am, the cops had been called to the Hadley household. The neighbors were fond of the family, but they were sick of the noise. Officers arrived at the scene and spoke with Tyler, who told them he'd make sure the noise stopped. As soon as the police car was out of sight, the music was cranked up again.

By 4 am, Tyler had been having so much fun he told everyone he was having another party that night.

Almost as soon as Tyler posted another invite on his social media page, the police were back at the door. Not due to the noise this time - but because Tyler's old friend Mike had called the police about the dead bodies in the bedroom.

"Are your parents home?" the officers asked Tyler, whose eyes were wide and his pupils huge. It was clear the teen had taken something. He was erratic, irritable, and not making much sense. The officers ordered Tyler to the floor and cuffed him. Then the teen said something strange; he told officers he knew he was going to jail, so they better just take him. When the police entered the house, the teenager became inconsolable, screaming at the officers that they couldn't go inside the house.

When they made it to the master bedroom, they broke the door down and discovered the disturbing allegations against Tyler were true. The teen was taken to the station while the party was shut down and swiftly turned into a crime scene.

A search of the house found Tyler's prescribed medications, anti-anxiety and antidepressants. The teen, after coming down from his ecstasy-induced state, would blame the pills he was prescribed for causing his murderous thoughts. Still, even when he was incarcerated while awaiting trial, he didn't show much remorse. In fact, he bragged about the party he held after committing the murders, telling one inmate, "You should have come, it was awesome."

Worse than this, he even gave himself his own killer name: "Hammer Time." He even began signing off his prison letters as "Hambo."

In 2014, Tyler was handed life in prison. Due to him being just shy of his 18th birthday when he committed the murders, Tyler was immune from the death penalty. It seems likely that life may mean life in this instance since Assistant State Attorney Tom Bakkedahl assured that the goal with Tyler's prison sentence wasn't rehabilitation but rather punishment for his crimes.

In letters to the friend who turned him in, Mike, Tyler says he's not the monster everyone thinks he is. In fact, he's a pretty nice guy: he's caring and simply made a horrible mistake.

It's a sad, senseless case that still has some big questions lingering as to what made Tyler want to end the lives of his parents in such a brutal way. Taking his phone away or stopping the teenager from driving their cars certainly isn't enough to drive him to murder his mother and father. Tyler was on medication, some of which was known to cause adverse effects in teenagers. He had also been given hormones from an early age, and you can only wonder what long-term effect this may have had on the growing boy's mental development. We may never know what caused this barbaric tragedy: nature, nurture, or the legal and illegal drugs used by Tyler Hadley.

In the spring of 2015, the Hadley family home was demolished.

Prejudice And Injustice

On September 10, 1982, the brutalized, beaten body of a man was discovered in Fairview Park, Dublin, Ireland. The still-warm body had been stripped of any belongings the man may have been carrying: cash, identification, or even house keys. The police were immediately called, and the fight was on to save his life.

Twenty-four hours earlier, 19-year-old Tony Maher was bored at home. He'd called in sick at work, but he wasn't bedbound. He'd merely hurt his foot, although his mother was convinced it was something serious like gangrene. The doctor assured the concerned mother that it was just a rash and that the teenager would be fine in a few days.

Tony wasn't someone who could sit around and do nothing, so after a few hours mulling around the house, he decided to head out and meet his girlfriend. The young couple then headed to Fairview Park, a lush area of greenery and wildlife where you might be lucky enough to spot some scurrying squirrels.

Fairview Park was one of Tony's main hangout areas. Sometimes, he and his gang of friends would play football there or bring cans of cheap cider to drink as the sun went down.

Not all of his extracurricular activities were so harmless, though. Sometimes, Tony and his pals would steal cars and drive them around until they were bored. Sometimes, they'd hang out in the park and look out for people they deemed to be homosexual. If someone was suspected to be gay, Tony and his crew would beat them up. The victim's "crime" was simply their perceived sexual orientation.

As well as beating up random men as they made their way through Fairview Park, the teenage group of friends would rob their victims of any cash they had. The youths viewed it as killing two birds with one stone. Tony was the oldest of his group, which consisted of 18-year-old Robert Armstrong, 18-year-old Patrick Kavanagh, 17-year-old Colm Donovan, and a 14-year-old boy who remains unnamed.

The gang of teens had recently been on a spree of "bashing" any men they presumed to be gay, tallying up over 20 victims over the course of six weeks. The teenagers didn't view their victims as such but rather saw them as deserving targets of their brutality. Should any of the men fight back against the gaggle of youths attacking them, the group made a point to really escalate the violence they inflicted on their victim. The year was 1982, and it was illegal to be gay in Ireland. It would take over a decade for this law to change.

While some of the group had jobs - Tony and Robert were in the army - the others just coasted by, causing trouble, and frittered their days away, engaging in antisocial activities. The same could be said for Tony and Robert, too. Their time in the army hadn't taught them much discipline, and when they were home, they'd reconnect with their wayward friends and get up to all kinds of criminal activities.

Robert and Tony were the closest out of the group. Robert had even moved in with Tony and his mother after being kicked out of his family home for his troubling behavior. Patrick and Colm's lack of direction also culminated in their antisocial behaviors, which were witnessed by the youngest in the group, a 14-year-old boy.

On the night of September 9, the gang all congregated at the park to make the most of the warm summer night. They met up with their girlfriends, chatting on the park benches and heckling at undeserving passersby. What else was there to do after all, except bother innocent people unlucky enough to be walking through Fairview Park at the same time the gang of youths were convened?

While I call them youths, it's important to note that two members of the group, Tony and Robert, were adults.

It was getting late, and the gang's girlfriends all decided to go home. Catherine, Tony's love interest, made her way home on her own. Sometimes, but not often, he'd walk her home when it was dark. Not tonight, though. You can only wonder: if Tony *had* decided to escort his girlfriend home that night, would you be reading about this case right now?

Shortly after the girls left for the night, the group of teens resumed chasing after men they presumed to be gay. One man got away, fleeing to a nearby road before the boys could grab him.

Meanwhile, 30-year-old Declan Flynn was finishing his night out at the Fairview Grill. He'd had a few pints at the pub with a friend before picking up some food at the grill, where he bumped into a friend. The pair talked for a short while before Declan made his way home through Fairview Park.

Declan was gay in a time and place where it was extremely dangerous to be your authentic self. His sexuality wasn't known to his family, but that didn't stop the young man from living the lifestyle he wanted. He would frequent gay bars and volunteer at a local gay community, although he kept this from those closest to him.

As the man made his way through Fairview Park, he decided to take a seat on one of the benches. By a stroke of great misfortune, he sat next to Patrick Kavanagh. The rest of the hateful group sat in the bushes, waiting for their moment to pounce on the man they suspected of being gay. They each found a suitable weapon, a tough branch or stick, and lay in anticipation for their time to strike.

"Get the bastard!" Patrick eventually yelled as he lunged at Declan, who managed to jump up and flee. The man raced through the park as fast as his feet would take him as the five boys chased him. Although Declan got a head start, the teenagers soon caught up with him and swung their weapons with enough force that they got their victim on the floor.

Heartbreakingly, Declan was mere feet away from the main road where the group's earlier victim managed to escape. In fact, you could see cars passing and hear the bustling of the customers exiting the Fairview Grill. Still, Declan's screams went unheard as the group of teens - including the 14-year-old boy - began raining blows down on their victim.

With their makeshift weapons and their feet, they beat Declan to a pulp. Once tired out, the five stood back to see the result of their violent actions. The victim was laid on his back, covered in blood. He was alive, just, but was clearly gasping for air. He was choking on his own blood. Tony could see the man was dying, so the group laid Declan on his side. They then fled the scene, leaving their victim to suffocate.

The group made a run for it until they found a quiet spot. Colm suggested that they may have beaten the guy a little too hard. The five, exasperated from running so fast, took the time to collect themselves and consider their next move. They knew the victim would be found - a call was placed to emergency services, which saw them arrive at the crime scene just before 2 a.m. the morning after the attack. Of all people, it was Robert Armstrong who dialed 999 to alert authorities.

Firefighters and paramedics were met with the still-warm body of a young man, his identity unknown since he carried no ID or any personal items. They rushed him to Blanchardstown Hospital in a bid to save his life, although no pulse was detected.

Meanwhile, the gang of youths had dispersed. The younger members all went home, while Tony and Robert went back to Tony's mother's house. The pair knew they'd just killed a man. He'd endured a barbaric beating by five people, and the amount of blood they saw pooling out of the man's mouth was like nothing they'd ever seen before. The victim was gasping for breath he couldn't take, and it was clear without help, the man would be dead in minutes.

Tony and Robert sat in silence for a while. Their thoughts were in sync: what's going to happen to us? No concern for the innocent man they'd beaten to death, just mere regard for themselves. "What's going to happen if they'll come for us?"

Robert asked, referring to the police. Tony didn't have an answer but wondered if the army would still let him serve. One thing Tony was certain of, however, was that he was keeping the barbaric events of September 10 to himself.

Other members of the gang weren't as tight-lipped, though. They'd already told their girlfriends the following day. The whole gang met up on the afternoon of September 11, and Tony wanted to make sure they were all on the same page to keep quiet. However, Robert brought an outsider along with him, so nobody could mention anything about the murder they'd committed the night before.

Robert's friend was known to the group but by no means was he close to them. In fact, Tony wasn't too keen on having him around, but he endured the man's company for the afternoon. Despite being an outsider, Robert's friend could sense some tension in the air among the group. They were all quiet, nervous, and taut. As the group walked towards the burger joint they'd agreed to grab lunch at, they passed a newsagent window. The murder of the man in Fairview Park was front-page news.

This visibly unsettled Robert and his friend noticed this. The unnamed friend suddenly put the puzzle pieces together. "You were the ones who killed the man," he said, not asked. Immediately, Robert shut him down, insisting none of them were anywhere near Fairview the night before. This didn't do much to convince Robert's friend, although he dropped the subject after the outraged reaction he received. The group ate their burgers, drank their milkshakes, and headed home.

Tony hadn't been able to talk to his friends about the killing. He needed to get it out, to talk to someone about it, so he asked his mother if she'd heard about it. He didn't get the response he was perhaps hoping for since his mother gave him a stern warning: he better have nothing to do with the murder. Tony vehemently denied being anywhere near the crime scene, insisting he'd been with his girlfriend all night.

Robert was also itching to get it off his chest. Since he couldn't speak to any of the others involved that afternoon, he decided to call his mother up and confess to her. She listened as her son admitted to beating a man to death. She called him an idiot. It's not clear whether she believed her son or not, but her reaction wasn't one of condemnation.

Word had gotten around pretty quickly, and just two days after the killing, the unnamed 14-year-old involved in the attack was arrested. He admitted he was part of the killing but stressed to the police that he only hit the victim with a branch once - it was the other, older boys who beat the man violently. The boy told investigators the names of all involved.

That early Sunday morning, when Tony heard a knock at the door, he knew the police had come for him. He waited for his dad to answer, which he did. Tony listened as his mother also raced to the door, asking officers what they wanted. The policemen couldn't tell the panicked mother why they were there, but they told her they'd be taking her son in for questioning. All Tony could think about was being locked up in jail. Still, he didn't deny the accusations investigators put in front of him. He admitted his role in the murder of the man in Fairview, who was now identified as Declan Flynn.

The others were swiftly arrested, too, and the confessions spilled from each.

Tony was able to pay bail, thanks to the generosity of his girlfriend's parents. Robert wasn't so lucky. It's unclear where Patrick and Colm went at this time - Colm was just 17, so jail wasn't an option. For Robert, though, he was locked up, contemplating his life being spent behind bars. For almost seven months, he awaited his trial. In March 1983, it arrived, and all five teenagers stood trial for the murder of Declan Flynn.

The courtroom was packed, the victim's family eager to see the killers face justice. But, the Flynn family would be dealt a heartbreaking blow.

"Five years on remand," the judge ordered. Tony was beside himself, turning to his mother. He couldn't handle five years in jail, he thought to himself. He asked his mother what the judge meant. She smiled at her son and told him the judge was letting him come home.

Tony Maher, Robert Armstrong, Patrick Kavanagh, Colm Donovan, and the unnamed 14-year-old boy all walked free that day despite being found guilty of manslaughter. "This could never be regarded as murder," the judge said when handing down the sentences, or lack thereof. It's hard to believe that just four decades ago, such prejudice and hatefulness were rewarded.

On December 1, 1987, Robert Armstrong was back before a judge. He and an accomplice had raped a pregnant woman in her own home. The wicked man gave the mother-to-be two choices: be kicked in the stomach or raped. He got 10 years in jail for this crime. You can but suggest that, if he'd been jailed for the murder of Declan Flynn, this horrific rape would never have taken place.

Declan's savage and untimely death would eventually receive the outrage it deserved years after his murder. As time went by, and as people's opinions changed, a new generation would commemorate Declan. In 2015, when the Marriage Equality referendum passed in Ireland, a bridge was embellished in his memory. The same day, the bench where Declan was accosted was adorned with flowers, notes, and decorations. People, many of whom weren't even alive when Declan was murdered, came to pay their respects and tell him how times have changed for the better.

Evil Desires

We often ponder what makes a serial killer. Upbringing, genetics, or a nasty injury to the head? Sometimes, we must consider that someone is *born* evil because that's the only explanation for their vile actions. This could be one such case.

Peter Dupas was born in New South Wales, Australia, in July 1953 to doting parents. His mother and father were older when they had Peter, and his siblings were much older than him. As such, little Peter grew up almost like the only child, enjoying the ample attention and time his parents could offer him. His upbringing was as normal and stable as you can hope any child would have. Peter was encouraged, nurtured, and given everything a growing child needs to do well in the world. Still, this wouldn't matter. As he entered his teens, Peter's desire to hurt women would become too strong for him to ignore.

In the autumn of 1968, aged just 15, Peter carried out his first known attack. It was a planned attack on a victim well-known to the boy, but that didn't stop him from choosing his next-door neighbor to mutilate.

The devious teenager knocked on the neighbor's door and asked if the woman would let him borrow a knife to prepare supper. The friendly woman let the teenager inside - why wouldn't she - and opened her cutlery drawer to hand the boy a sharp knife. Little did she know, she was handing Peter a weapon to be used against her.

As the woman was telling Peter what a good boy he was for helping his mother prepare food, he plunged the knife into her stomach. The wounded victim fell to the floor, and the bloodthirsty teenager climbed on top of her and began stabbing her face and neck, piercing through her hands as she tried to protect herself. Once he was done with the knife, Peter began banging his victim's head off the floor. Then, almost suddenly, the boy just stopped. He got off the badly wounded, terrified woman and left.

The police were called, and Peter didn't deny the horrific attack. He admitted he did it but couldn't remember much past having the knife in his hand. For this violent crime, the boy was given a year and a half of probation and sent to a psychiatric hospital for further evaluation. It was determined the pressure he felt he was under from his parents pushed him to lash out viciously. He was sent home after a fortnight.

Almost exactly a year later, Austin Hospital, Melbourne, was broken into. The mortuary on site was the main target for the intruder, who'd found a pathologist's knife and had mutilated some of the corpses that were stored there. Nobody was ever caught for this sick crime, although one individual would later become a prime suspect - Peter Dupas.

As the years passed and Peter became an adult, his twisted predilections wouldn't disappear. In the spring of 1972, aged 19, he was caught peeking through someone's window. He caught glimpses of a woman taking a shower until the unsuspecting female's husband spotted the peeping tom and chased him away. The following year, another complaint about

Peter was rung into the local police station. A motorist had jotted down Peter's license plate number after they spotted the driver smirking and smiling at their 12-year-old daughter in an inappropriate way.

In November 1973, the perverse man struck again, this time carrying out a horrifying attack on a good samaritan. A woman spotted a man outside her home, pacing back and forth beside his car. She headed out to ask him if he was okay, and he replied his car had broken down. After discussing what may be wrong with the vehicle, the woman went back inside to get a screwdriver for the man.

Peter snuck into the house behind the woman and hid. While hiding, he found a knife. When he saw an opportunity, he lunged toward his victim with the weapon and threatened to kill her and her unborn baby using the knife. He then proceeded to rape the terrified woman.

The break-in and assault was eerily similar to a few that had taken place in recent weeks, although the other female victims hadn't been raped. The attacker had attempted to sexually assault one victim, but she warned the man that her husband was due home any minute, so the criminal fled.

Eventually, Peter was arrested under suspicion of rape. However, investigators found the man extremely frustrating to extract information from. The suspect's tactic was to deny everything presented to him, even in the face of irrefutable evidence. The investigating officers noted that Peter came across as weak in the face of authority and hoped this might go some way in helping them secure a confession. Sometimes, under intense interrogation, it would seem like officers were on the brink of getting a confession from Peter. However, he would always backtrack and shut down if he found himself getting to the point of admitting guilt.

Still, Peter was charged with rape and was let out on bail. However, part of his bail condition was to remain at Mont Park Psychiatric Hospital, although he was free to leave the premises whenever he pleased. This would allow the serial sex offender to strike again. The hospital was close to a beach, which Peter would frequent. He wouldn't sunbathe or take a dip in the sea, though; he'd make his way to the ladies' showers and hide in a cubicle to watch unsuspecting girls as they washed the sand off their bodies.

After multiple occasions, the police finally caught Peter in the act and trapped him in the female toilets before he could flee the scene. He was taken back to Mont Park and ordered to stay there.

In the summer of 1974, Peter was finally sentenced for the burglary and rape he committed the year prior. He was handed nine years behind bars, with a minimum of five years to be served.

By 1979, Peter was back on the streets after serving just over five and a half years. After just two months of freedom, he began attacking women yet again, embarking on a 10-day spree of depravity. It seems prison did nothing for Peter except give him time to plan his next attacks. This time around, he donned a balaclava and made sure to bring his own knife with him.

One woman was raped in a public toilet at knifepoint. Three more were also attacked, two of whom managed to flee the sexual assault. The third woman was stabbed in her chest, but she still fought off her attacker, who gave up and raced away from the scene. Naturally, the police suspected the sex attacker on the loose was Peter Dupas since all the attacks occurred shortly after his stint in prison. As soon as they picked him up, Peter admitted his guilt. When asked why he attacks women, he simply shrugged it off as an "urge." He also tried to suggest he was acting out because his ex had left him, and because he was a loner.

Again, Peter was charged with rape and assault. You'd think that this time around, the sentence would be harsher. In fact, it was lighter than his previous sentencing - he got six and a half years in jail.

Fast forward to early 1985, and Peter is back on the streets yet again. Less than a week after his release for rape, predictably, he struck again. A 21-year-old woman was sunbathing on Blairgowrie Beach, Victoria, the same beach Peter was lying on. The lone woman caught the predator's eye, and he pounced on her and raped her. After the attack, he fled the scene but struggled to remember where he'd parked his car.

By this point, the woman had dressed herself and found two men walking near the beach. She told them what had happened, and they took off in search of the rapist. Sure enough, they found the man wandering around looking for his car. The police were called, and again, Peter was hauled in for another rape charge. He admitted his guilt but chillingly told investigators that he "couldn't help himself." Peter also expressed the desire to live a normal life and said he was sorry for the attack. It seems neither statement was true, nor was it likely believed by the officers interviewing him.

While officers had Peter in their custody, they asked him about the unsolved murder of a sunbather a fortnight prior. Although Peter was still technically incarcerated on this date, the day the woman was murdered coincided with Peter's day leave from jail. The mother was brutally and violently beaten to death and left in the sand dunes of Rye Beach, Victoria. Peter insisted he had nothing to do with the killing.

By the time Peter's trial came about, the rapist wasn't as lucky as he had been previously. Judge Leo Lazarus had handed Peter just over five years for his spate of rapes and assaults, something Judge John Leckie described as "inadequate." This time, the judge was going to make sure the sentence wasn't as paltry and doubled it to 12 years in jail.

It was ordered that Peter sought treatment for his sexual deviancy while in jail, and he did undergo treatment that was supposed to quell his sex drive. When his release came around in the spring of 1992, it seemed this would truly test the mettle of the rehabilitation program.

It had failed. Within 18 months of his release, Peter attacked a young girl riding her horse. The 15-year-old managed to outsmart her attacker by using the horse as a shield before running away. In January 1994, he was again wearing a balaclava and carrying a knife. That month, he burst into a public toilet, pulled his balaclava over his face, and pulled out his weapon. He then broke down the cubicle door of a 26-year-old who was using the restroom. Terrified at the sight before her - the chubby frame of a man wearing a black mask with eye holes cut out - she screamed. The man began pointing a knife at the woman, who defied her attacker's commands to face the wall.

For her lack of compliance, Peter began stabbing the woman, who put her hands up to defend herself. Injured and her arms dripping with blood, she fought back against the man trying to drag her from the cubicle. Then, suddenly, her attacker just stopped. He let her go and walked away calmly. This echoes Peter's first known attack as a 15-year-old boy, where he halted the attack on his neighbor and left like nothing had happened.

Peter didn't know that the woman's husband was an off-duty police officer. After the attack, the distraught woman raced to her spouse and described her attacker to him. Filled with rage, the man rounded up his friends, and they set out looking for the man. They eventually found Peter and ran his car off the road. Yet again, he found himself in handcuffs at the wrong end of the interrogation table.

He got just over a year in jail for this twisted crime. By September 1996, the serial sex pest was back on the streets *again*. Perhaps you already know what's coming, but it seems the judicial system hadn't entirely worked out the pattern yet.

Just over a year later, toward the end of 1997, a spate of attacks were carried out on women. The first was a sex worker named Margaret Maher, on October 4.

She was found by aluminum collectors as they searched a junk pile. Margaret had been left under some cardboard boxes. She'd been beaten and stabbed, with wounds to her wrists. Barbarically, her left breast had been cut off. The killer then inexplicably put it in the victim's mouth.

Just a month later, 25-year-old Mersina Halvagis was murdered after being stabbed ferociously as she visited her grandmother's grave. As she kneeled down to lay a bunch of flowers atop the grave, the violent killer snuck up behind her and ended her life.

Then, on New Year's Eve morning, 1997, 95-year-old Kathleen Downes was just waking up. She lived at Brunswick Lodge nursing home since she struggled to walk as a result of two strokes. The frail woman endured a horrific death at the hands of a sadistic killer who broke into the nursing home and stabbed her to death.

Just over a year passed, and on the evening of April 19, 1999, psychotherapist Nicole Patterson was found dead at her home office. She worked from home and saw many of her clients there. Could it be that one of them snapped and murdered their therapist?

The 28-year-old was naked from the waist down. Her friend noticed that while Nicole had blood on her, she looked clean somehow; there were no pools of blood surrounding her despite her body being full of stab wounds. It was almost as if someone had tried to tidy up the area of any evidence. Disturbingly, both of Nicole's breasts had been removed, but they weren't at the crime scene. It seemed the killer had taken them as a memento.

The autopsy revealed the young woman had suffered nearly 30 stab wounds in total, so it was difficult to work out which one was the fatal injury.

Officers couldn't help but notice that the removal of the breasts was similar to an unsolved murder from years ago - the brutal killing of Margaret Maher.

Inspecting the crime scene, investigators noted that the killer had cleaned up after themselves meticulously. There were no fingerprints, footprints, or DNA left by the culprit. They'd wiped everything down thoroughly. However, they'd neglected to consider any evidence Nicole may have unwittingly left posthumously.

In her planner was a 9 am appointment that day for a man named Malcolm. It had "Malcolm's" number alongside the time slot. This led police to trace the cell number to a student who had no idea about Nicole or any therapy session. He had let someone else use his phone lately, though - Peter Dupas, for whom he was doing handy work.

For Peter to do something so despicable wasn't out of the realm of possibility. In fact, it was more likely than not the man had reoffended since his release from jail, although police were unsure if he was a cold-blooded murderer.

A subsequent raid of Peter's home found a bloodstained jacket of his, a balaclava, and a newspaper article reporting on Nicole's murder. Officers also noticed the suspect had defensive scratch marks on his face. The police seized the soiled jacket and ran DNA testing on the blood. One of the blood droplets belonged to Peter.

The other 13 belonged to Nicole Patterson.

If that wasn't enough evidence, Peter had left a trail of calls to Nicole in the weeks leading up to her murder and mutilation. He used these calls to gauge his prey's vulnerability; speaking to her under the guise of being a prospective client.

Still, the unrepentant man wouldn't confess to the police. He claimed his face injuries were from a DIY project where he accidentally hit himself with a piece of wood. Peter couldn't argue with the scientific evidence against him, though, and was charged with murder.

In August 2000, he was handed life in jail. More importantly, unlike previous sentences, the opportunity for him to be released was revoked. By this point, it would be almost certain that the man would strike again if ever let out. Naturally, Peter has tried to appeal his sentence, clearly exposing his lack of awareness over the severity and barbarity of his crimes. His attempts were shut down.

That wouldn't be the end of the story, though. The police knew Peter had committed more than just one murder and were intent on making sure the victims received justice.

They took his DNA sample and cross-referenced it to a black glove they found at Margaret Maher's body. It was Peter's DNA.

This then led investigators on a hunt to tie Peter to more victims. He was heavily suspected in the murder of Mersina Halvagis, who was killed while paying respects to her late grandparent. They managed to compile quite the list of evidence against Peter - nine different people saw Peter at the cemetery that day. Peter's grandfather's grave is close to where Mersina was killed. The suspect had changed his appearance directly after Mersina's body was found. Around the time of the murder, Peter had been seen with facial injuries, perhaps as a result of defensive scratches.

All of this was circumstantial, though. It wouldn't hold up in court. Until in 2002, when Peter admitted to killing the woman to a fellow inmate. This led to murder charges being brought against Peter, who denied any wrongdoing. It took until 2007 for his sentencing to take place, where he was found guilty of another murder and given another life sentence.

There was a spate of other violent sexual assaults and murders that occurred when Peter was on day release from jail or not in prison. These include the woman beaten to death on Rye Beach and a store owner who was murdered in her shop with a knife. Both attacks matched Peter's MO.

Kathleen Downes, the elderly lady who was killed on New Year's Eve in 1997, is another crime Peter is suspected of carrying out. Not only was she stabbed in the same way as the other victims, but Peter had been making calls to Brunswick Lodge nursing home in the weeks leading up to the woman's murder. The man knew nobody there, and there wasn't any reason for him to be calling. He was charged with her murder in 2018 and is awaiting sentencing.

Currently, Peter moves between two high-security prisons in Melbourne, Australia. He's never expressed remorse, regret, or one ounce of guilt for his actions. If you had to surmise what an evil sexual predator is, then Peter Dupas is the best living example you could think of.

Beyond Recognition

Despite humans being evolved creatures, some of us still exhibit primitive behaviors. Some people are outraged at the idea that other humans dare to be different from themselves and make it known as much. Sophie Lancaster was an individual who you could describe as "alternative" and she dressed in the gothic subculture style.

For this, she brutally lost her life at the hands of a mob who disapproved of her style of clothing. To reread that sentence back feels too nonsensical to be true.

She brutally lost her life at the hands of a mob who disapproved of her style of clothing.

But, sadly, the murder of Sophie Lancaster is very real, and so is the senseless "reason" she lost her life.

Sophie was born in Lancashire, England, in November 1986 to Sylvia and John Lancaster. The family adored the happy baby, including her older brother Adam. As Sophie grew up, she was known to be shy and introverted but incredibly sweet and sensitive. Throughout school, the girl was noted as being bright with a special interest in English language.

As she entered her teens, Sophie began taking an interest in gothic subculture. She wore dark, punky clothing, donned black eyeliner, and, over the years, added many piercings to her face. It was a look she used to express herself, just like any other group in school. You have the gym kids in their sportswear, the skater kids in their slouchy jeans, and the arty kids in their hipster-inspired outfits. Each clique had its own uniform, so to speak, and Sophie really resonated with the gothic-style clothing of the subculture.

The teen would meet like-minded individuals, including Robert Maltby, who would become her boyfriend. Just like Sophie, Robert was kind, quiet, and sensitive. The pair shared a love of all things gothic, similar music interests, and were both creative individuals. However, the look the couple donned would often cause other teens to pick on them and hurl abuse their way. Sophie and Robert would ignore such unwarranted nastiness, choosing to walk past their tormentors without rising to their hate-filled insults.

The couple's relationship was more than just a teenage fling. Before long, three years had passed, and the pair were as happy as ever, planning their future together. By this point, Sophie was 20, and Robert was 21. The couple had been described as "soulmates" by mutual friends who were sure the pair would spend the rest of their lives together. Sophie aspired to obtain an English degree, a subject she excelled at and took great interest in. Sadly, she'd never have the chance to go to university.

On August 11, 2007, Sophie and Robert walked home through Stubbylee Park. The area was surrounded by woodland and children's play areas and was home to a pond and lots of wildlife. It was the perfect location for a wholesome afternoon stroll or a picnic in the daytime.

By nightfall, however, the area could turn sinister. As the saying goes, the freaks come out at night, and some of them would assemble at Stubbylee Park after the sun goes down. On this particular evening, the "freaks" were a gang of teenagers hell-bent on tormenting any "goths" and "moshers" they came across. It was just past 1 am, and Ryan Herbert, Brendan Harris, Daniel Mallett, and siblings Joseph and Danny Hulme were hanging out at the Stubbylee Park gates.

The group of boys spotted the alternative duo, dressed in mostly black with their plethora of piercings. Neither Sophie nor Robert acknowledged the gang of youths, nor did they react when the boys began yelling obscenities at the pair. The couple were used to some people saying mean things about their appearance; they'd sadly accepted it as part of being "different." As the young couple made their way past the heckling teenagers, the lack of response clearly irritated the baying boys.

The gang began trailing the couple, repeating their awful insults and trying to provoke a reaction. When one wasn't offered, the group attacked Robert from behind, punching and kicking the man until he collapsed to the floor. Sophie was screaming and yelling for the youths to get off her boyfriend, although they took no heed of her pleas. In desperation, Sophie draped herself over her bloodied partner in an effort to shield him from the vicious kicks he was getting in the face and head.

The gang didn't relent, though. Instead, they turned their barbaric attentions to Sophie and began beating and kicking her in the head and body, stomping on her petite frame, laughing as they did. One boy even used both feet to jump up and down on the defenseless woman's head.

The attack was witnessed by some other teens, who called for an ambulance. As the call was made to 999, the gang of boys fled the scene, upbeat about the attack they'd just carried out. When the group encountered other friends, they gleefully told them what they'd done to the "moshers" at the park. "We did something good; you should have seen them - they were a right mess," one of the boys was overheard saying.

An ambulance eventually got to Stubbylee Park, although the paramedics struggled to make out where the victims were in the park due to how dark it was. When they found the badly injured pair, their faces had been beaten so badly they couldn't work out which victim was male and which one was female.

The couple were still alive - just. Due to the darkness and area they were in, the paramedics couldn't work to save the victims' lives in the park; they had to be rushed to hospital. Before being carried to the ambulance, the police arrived on the scene and searched the victims for identification. They could only find the ID of Robert Maltby. The couple were each put into a coma at Fairfield General Hospital, and police officers had the task of letting Robert's loved ones know the heartbreaking news.

They arrived at his parent's house and advised them their son had been brutally attacked. They also asked who the female he was with could be. Robert was always with Sophie, so they told officers it was most likely his girlfriend. The Maltby parents passed on Sophie's details, and the police headed to the Lancaster family home.

Sylvia Lancaster woke up early on the morning of August 12 and made herself busy by having an early gym session and picking up some groceries. Upon returning home, she found someone had posted a card through the letterbox. It was from the police, asking Sylvia to get in touch. Naturally, the mother was panicked, but never in a million years would she guess that her daughter had been beaten into a coma. She raced to the landline.

Picking up the receiver, she was notified she had 14 new messages on her answering machine. This panicked Sylvia even more - she knew something truly horrible had happened. Before she could hurriedly listen to the voicemails - all left within the space of an hour - a call came through from her son Adam. "Sophie's in a coma. She's been attacked," he said. Sylvia could barely believe what she was hearing.

Meanwhile, Stubbylee Park had been cordoned off and was now a bustling crime scene. The pools of blood from the victims stained the concrete floor, piles of used beer cans sat nearby, along with smashed bottles. Somebody, somewhere, knows who did this, and the police were going to make sure they found out who.

Sylvia and Adam raced to the hospital to be by Sophie's side. As they made their way into intensive care, they were met with the beaten, disfigured face of Sophie - but they didn't recognize her. She'd been attacked so brutally that she didn't look like her anymore. Purple bruises covered her face, head, ears, and down her neck. Parts of her hair were missing. Tubes were coming out of her mouth and nose. Her eyelids were purple and yellow and swollen. There were more injuries they couldn't see beneath the robe she was wearing.

News spread around the local area, but nobody came forward with any information. Then, as the days passed, some good news finally arrived: Robert was making some progress. Eventually, he came out of his coma, and although he had little recollection of the events, it looked like he had a good chance at recovery. Sadly, the same couldn't be said for Sophie. It was acknowledged by hospital staff that the young woman would likely never come out of her coma.

In an unusual turn of events, a forensic pathologist was sent to Sophie's bedside while she was still alive to determine the cause and extent of the injuries she suffered. Investigators didn't want a shred of evidence to pass them by, and with it looking like the worst possible outcome for Sophie, they needed to document as much as they could while they could. The pathologist was able to determine that Sophie had been kicked in the head multiple times by more than one person.

The hunt was on for the attackers.

By August 27, Sophie had been declared brain dead. Her mother knew the inevitable was going to happen, and the night before Sophie died, Sylvia stayed by her bedside and fixed her child's hair. It was the only part of her daughter she could touch; the rest of her was covered in wires and machinery.

The life support was turned off, and the hunt for Sophie's attackers had been escalated to the hunt for her murderers.

The decision was made that since the killers were likely youths, older investigators on the case wouldn't be able to build rapport with anyone who could point them in the right direction. As a result, they'd be less likely to extract valuable evidence from potential witnesses. In a bold move by the lead investigator, young and inexperienced officers were placed on the case and sent out to interview those who'd been in or around the park that night.

The move paid off, although it could have gone either way. After speaking to hundreds of possible leads, one young girl admitted she'd seen the attack and gave the young interviewing officer five names.

Ryan Herbert, Brendan Harris, Daniel Mallett, Joseph Hulme, and Danny Hulme were brought in for questioning.

Brendan Harris was keen to separate himself from the attack on Sophie. He admitted taking part in Robert Maltby's assault but told officers that the beating Sophie endured was carried out solely by Ryan Herbert. He described how Ryan forcefully kicked the young woman in the back of the head as she lay on the floor. Brendan also noted that Ryan called Sophie a "witness" to the assault and had to be dealt with.

Ryan Herbert, when confronted with this, repeated "no comment" throughout his interview. Still, his footwear had been taken for examination, and the results were indisputable. Sophie's blood, along with Robert's, was spattered all over the soles of his sneakers. Ryan, along with Brendan, were held in police custody. The three remaining boys were let out on bail.

March 2008 rolled around, and the murder trial began. All five boys pleaded guilty to grievous bodily harm with intent, but only Ryan pleaded guilty to murder. Brendan denied murder, still insisting only Ryan attacked Sophie.

While deliberating the teenager's guilt, the jury was told the violent motivation for the attack was the group's dislike of the clothing the victims wore. Sophie and Robert had never done anything to any of the boys who attacked them, yet they were mercilessly beaten by them regardless.

There was also more evidence against Ryan - a recorded phone call to his mother while he was detained in a youth offending prison awaiting trial. His mother advised him not to worry about jail since he hadn't done anything. It was at this point

Ryan admitted he *had* been involved in Sophie's murder. Even more damning was a bugged conversation between Ryan and Brandan, where Ryan joked about kicking the victim's head "like a football."

Ryan and Brendan both got life in jail for their part in Sophie's murder. The jury didn't accept that Brendan didn't play a significant role in Sophie's death, and he was found guilty of her murder alongside Ryan.

Joseph Hulme, Danny Hulme, and Daniel Mallett were all found guilty of grievous bodily harm with intent for their attack on Robert. The Hulme brothers got five years and ten months, while Mallett got four years and four months in prison.

Surprisingly, out of all the boys jailed, the one who appeared to make the most progress was Ryan Herbert. Brendan got extra years added to his sentence for breaking a nurse's nose while Ryan was taking strides toward obtaining a degree and working on his interpersonal skills. His notable improvement even saw the criminal - by now a man - allowed days out of jail. It was announced in 2022 that Ryan would be released from prison, a decision that Sylvia Lancaster condemned.

In the years after her child's untimely and senseless death, Sylvia made it her mission to ensure her daughter was never forgotten. She started the Sophie Lancaster Foundation, a charity offering educational workshops that challenge prejudice and narrow-mindedness towards people considered "alternative" or "different." Sylvia also worked with a popular British soap opera on a storyline that mirrored the tragic tale of her daughter. In 2014, the mother received an OBE for her relentless work in reducing hate crime.

Sylvia Lancaster OBE sadly died in 2022 due to complications arising after surgery. She was 69 years old and had spent the previous fifteen years campaigning for a more tolerant society. In doing so, Sylvia left the world in a much better state than how she found it, particularly for her Lancashire community.

After Sophie's death, Robert Maltby struggled to get by. He plunged into a deep depression and refused to visit his late girlfriend's grave. He would shy away from interviews and speaking to the media, insisting that the "goth angle" they spun was simplistic. Robert said the attack was the result of a much bigger social issue.

He has since found love again and no longer relates to the gothic subculture.

Twisted Revenge

The crime I'm about to cover happened almost 100 years ago. It took place over a tense, angst-filled week, which saw the city of Los Angeles praying for the safe return of 12-year-old Marion Parker. The girl had been kidnapped and held at ransom for a large sum of money, with her abductor threatening the child's life if $1,500 wasn't handed over in exchange for her safe return.

There have been many violent crimes carried out in Los Angeles over the years, some disturbingly gory and gruesome. The Black Dahlia always comes to my mind when I think of Hollywood and its history of disturbing murders. This case ranks up there as being just as vile, if not more, as the Dahlia killing.

The tale of Marion Parker, despite it taking place almost a century ago, is still remembered due to its shocking brutality and the callousness of the perpetrator.

It was the lead-up to Christmas in California. Although decorations adorned shop windows, candy canes hung from trees, and the excitement of Santa arriving filled the air, the warm weather didn't quite match the christmassy spirit. Still, the school year was almost ending, and Marion Parker couldn't wait to enjoy the festive season with her twin sister.

On December 15, a smartly dressed, well-kept, well-spoken young man turned up at Marion's school. He told staff members that Perry Parker had sent him to collect his daughter. "Which daughter?" the school official asked. "The younger one," the unknown man smiled. Naturally, this didn't sit right with the employee - the girls were twins, and there was no younger one. When the man was presented with this information, he quickly corrected himself: he was sent for the *smaller* girl.

Of course, the man's lack of knowledge of the girls alarmed the school assistant and he sensed this. "I work with Perry Parker at the bank. He's been involved in an accident - please call the bank to confirm this," the man suggested. The employee took the stranger at his word and gave him what he requested: Marion Parker.

The man fled with the girl. By the time school finished, and only Majorie Parker arrived home, the Parker parents began to worry. Her sister had no idea where Marion was. The girl was reported missing.

By this point, the kidnapper had a good few hours head start on the search party. He'd fled through Hollywood, driving the girl through the hills and taking her to his home.

There were no leads, no evidence trail, and nothing police could go off aside from the description of the man who'd taken Marion. Still, LA's a big place, and it would take time to finalize the sketch of the suspect. Then, it would need to be sent to the newspapers for them to write up their story and print a plea for witnesses. Time was ticking and it wasn't on Marion's side.

Before any of this could happen, Perry Parker received two telegrams. One originated from Pasadena and the other from Alhambra, both just a 15-minute drive from each other. It seemed as if the kidnapper was trying to throw the Parker family off his scent. In the telegram signed off by a "George Fox," the man demanded $1,500 from Perry. Other telegrams stated that Perry shouldn't dare try to sabotage the exchange or else his daughter's life would be ended. It was already hanging by a thread, the telegram warned. In fact, the kidnapper cautioned, he had a razor at hand ready to execute the girl.

More telegrams arrived over the next few hours, this time signed off in Greek. One letter was signed as "Death," and another had "Fate" at the foot of the letter. Still, the demands remained the same: the abductor wanted his $1,500 in $20 gold certificates and wanted them hand-delivered by Perry Parker.

Included in the demands was something to provoke emotion and quick action from the Parker family: a handwritten note from Marion. In the letter, she told her parents that the man had told her he'd kill her and begged her father to let her come home.

Perry hurriedly did as the abductor demanded, gathering the money together. However, despite being in a heightened state of anxiety, the father still had his wits about him. While compiling the bank notes, he made a note of each of their serial numbers. This, in theory, would lead the police back to the kidnapper when he used them in the future.

As the sun went down on December 16, Perry received a phone call from the man who had his daughter. He told the father where to meet him and advised him how the exchange would occur: money first. Then he'd let Marion run over to her family. Perry stacked the notes in a suitcase and headed out to get his daughter back.

The Parker family had been liaising with the LAPD prior to the meeting, and officers swarmed the rendezvous area in an attempt to snare the kidnapper. However, they didn't make their presence subtle, and the kidnapper spotted them scouring the area. Perry waited at the agreed meeting point, but the man never showed. Instead, he sent Perry another telegram, scolding him for involving the police. In the same letter, he warned the man that there was only one day left before the deal was off completely, and he'd kill little Marion.

For the next meet-up, the man warned Perry he would be "two billion times more cautious and clever and deadly" than before. He then warned the father that only God, not law enforcement, could help him. Inserted in the communication was another letter from Marion, begging her father not to involve the police.

Perry set out to meet the kidnapper at 7:30 pm on December 17. They stood face to face on the corner of 5th Avenue and South Manhattan Street, where Marion's abductor held a gun toward Perry. "You know what I'm here for," the criminal said. Of course, Perry knew why he was standing opposite the thin, serious man pointing a shotgun at him. "Can I see my girl?" Perry replied.

The gun-wielding man pointed towards his car, where Marion was clearly visible in the window of the passenger side. "Marion!" her father cried, although the girl didn't respond. The closer Perry looked, the more he could see his daughter's eyes; they were wide open and not blinking. She just stared straight past him. He thought this was the effects of drugging and that his daughter was in a comatose state.

Perry handed the money over, and as promised, the assailant gave the distressed father his daughter. He opened his passenger door and pushed the little girl out of the car as he sped off. "There's your daughter!" he yelled. The girl was wrapped up like a package to her neck. Perry raced over to his child and held her. She was dead. He let out a shriek that could be heard blocks away. Her wide-open eyes had been held in place with piano wires.

The police arrived, and the little girl's body was taken away for autopsy that night. It was estimated the child had been dead for around twelve hours. Marion's arms and legs had been cut off. She'd also been disemboweled, and her stomach had a man's shirt stuffed inside it. The girl's back had been flogged so violently the skin was hanging off. Her throat had been slashed.

The cause of death wasn't ascertained, although it was made clear the child's death wasn't quick nor painless. In fact, she could very well have been alive as her limbs were chopped from her body.

Whoever had done this was undeniably twisted, and he had the edge over law enforcement. They'd avoided the exchange of money to ensure Marion's safe return. They had no clue where the murderer had raced off to.

The next day, a man out walking stumped upon something disturbing: little limbs wrapped in newspaper. The police were called, and it was confirmed the arms and legs belonged to Marion. A reward of $50,000 was put up for anyone who could bring the killer to justice. It was the 20s - whether he was alive or dead didn't matter. All that mattered was that the evil perpetrator was brought to justice.

Perry described the man as early to mid-20s, small framed, around 150 pounds if he were to guess, and about 5 foot 8. Dark-haired, clean-shaven, and with delicate features, the father had painted a thorough image of the killer.

The hunt was on, and a new clue quickly excited investigators at the prospect of nailing the killer. The shirt found in Marion's stomach had a laundry mark that led officers to the Bellevue Arms apartments. The police raided the apartment block, bursting into each room to apprehend whoever may look like the suspect. They stormed into the room of a man named Donald Evans, a dark-haired man who'd been sleeping.

The man was shocked to find the police in his apartment and even more stunned to find out why they were there. "I hope you catch that fiend," he said as officers explained the macabre murder of Marion. No clues were found in Donald's place, so investigators moved on to the next apartment.

A break came shortly after when the stolen car the murderer used was found abandoned. It contained the fingerprints of known criminal William Hickman. Finally, a trial to follow, officers thought. When the police presented this fresh information to Perry, a connection was made between the pair. William had previously worked at the same bank where Perry was a cashier. Not only that, William had been fired for forging checks. Perry Parker had been the one to testify against William at his trial, suggesting that the former employee serve jail time for his crimes. That's exactly what happened.

By now, William Hickman's mugshot was on the front page of newspapers not just in LA but across the country.

Upon seeing the mugshot, Donald Evans' landlady approached the police. Donald and William were the same person. Unknowingly, the police had come face to face with the killer and let him go.

"Donald" had fled the Bellevue Arms apartments by this point. A full search of his room was carried out, and blood was found in his apartment.

The leading hope officers had was that William would spend some of the money he'd been given, the serial numbers of which had been noted. By December 21, the killer would use one of the notes in Seattle. The following day, he used another in Portland, Oregon, and the police caught up with him, finally arresting him for the murder of Marion Parker.

Surprisingly, a confession was made immediately - although it wasn't truthful. William said he had kidnapped the girl, but he wasn't the one who killed her. He even offered officers a name - but the man William accused of murder was in jail at the time Marion was killed.

When asked why he kidnapped the child, William said he was trying to raise money for college. This was dismissed as lies, and it was suggested the real reason he chose Marion was to get revenge on her father, who'd helped send him to jail previously. The more investigators dealt with William, the more they began to think he simply wanted the attention and notoriety that the high-profile crime attracted.

Wily, sneaky, and unrepentant, William began plotting his defense while in custody. He even asked a prison guard how a crazy person would act: the criminal was setting the foundations for an insanity plea.

He also began divulging more information about Marion's murder, perhaps in a bid to aid him with his plea. William admitted to killing the girl in his Bellevue Arms apartment. He said he strangled her until she was seemingly unconscious before taking her to the bathroom. He tied the girl by her feet over the bathtub and slashed her throat. He then cut the girl's limbs off. Afterward, he disemboweled her. As the girl's innards were collecting in the bathtub, William said the girl awoke, her body flailing with such force she got herself out of the tub.

The injuries were unsurvivable.

After cleaning up, William said he wrapped Marion's arms and legs in paper and hid her body in a suitcase. Inexplicably, he then headed out to catch a movie. Returning home, he realized he might not get the ransom without showing Perry his daughter. So, in a bid to make the girl look alive, he used makeup on her pale face and taped her eyes open with piano keys. The despicable killer dared to claim the girl didn't suffer throughout her ordeal.

The murder trial took place in January 1928. William had been setting up his defense in the weeks prior, and his attorney used a new law to get his client off the hook: mental illness. Just a year before, a new bill passed that meant those suffering from mental illness couldn't be responsible for their actions.

Various psychiatrists had analyzed William, all of whom deemed the man sane. It was also noted the killer had been telling people the judge in his case wouldn't send him to death since he didn't believe in capital punishment. This was proven wrong when the judge did, in fact, sentence him to death for the murder of Marion Parker. Surprisingly, William took this well. "The state won by a neck," he smiled when asked about his thoughts on the sentencing.

In the fall of that year, William Hickman was led to the gallows. He'd had nine months in jail to repent and show real remorse, neither of which he truly did. He did write letters to the Parker family seeking forgiveness, and apparently, he found religion. However, his last words weren't omissions of guilt or repentance but rather concern as to where he would be buried.

The noose was tied around the killer's neck, and he fell to his death through the trap doors of the gallows. He didn't die instantly. Instead of his neck snapping, William hung, slowly suffocating to death as the thick rope deprived him of oxygen. The man jerked violently for two minutes as life dimmed from his eyes.

By no means a quick or painless death, but still nowhere near as torturous as the one Willaim Edward Hickman carried out on Marion Parker.

Dungeon Beneath The Cellar

I've covered a few "captives in the basement" crimes over the past few installments of this series. It's a disturbing subcategory of true crime cases whereby a victim, more often than not female, is abducted and kept in the captor's cellar. Usually, the victim or victims are sexually assaulted. Sometimes, the captives are released when the criminal is done with them. Sometimes, the victim finds a way to escape. And sometimes, the only way the captive leaves their prison is in a body bag.

The case of Li Hao is one of these "captive in the basement" stories, and this tale takes us to Henan, China, in the late noughties.

Very little is known about Li Hao prior to his crimes, but the little information available suggests the 35-year-old man had a 24-year-old wife and a son under one when he carried out his spate of abductions.

Li had a respectable job working at the Technological Supervision Bureau in Luoyang and was a fireman before this. He had an honorable life, a life that many of his peers could only aspire to have. Still, Li had some dark perversions and, in the autumn of 2009, set out to make his fantasies a reality.

He'd recently bought a residential compound, unbeknown to his wife, to keep women there. He plotted for over a year, building a tunnel in the cellar. The tunnel would lead to his "dungeon," where he would keep his "slaves." The narrow tunnel was four feet beneath the basement and consisted of two tiny rooms, each barely big enough to fit a single bed. Still, Li managed to kit the rooms with the most basic amenities. There was no toilet or cleaning facilities, just a makeshift bed for a small sliver of comfort for whoever may dwell there.

For over 12 months, the man worked to build his hidden torture den, acutely aware of what he was going to use it for once it was completed. Li had over a year to come to his senses before he committed crimes he could never undo, but the man didn't want to; he was adamant he was going to abduct women and keep them for his own twisted wants. In fact, he even went to the trouble of fortifying the dungeon by securing no less than seven doors to prevent any unwanted escapes.

As well as abusing the women himself, Li had plans to make money from the victims. He decided he'd force the women into performing live shows for viewers online, although Li would be the one to profit from their misery.

Once the subterranean cellar within a cellar was finished, there was just one more thing Li had to do: capture his victims. He thought of places he could find the most vulnerable women who'd fit his criteria. In the end, he decided karaoke bars would be his best bet in finding his future captives.

By the end of 2009, he had two women in his dungeon: Zhang and Duan. He'd lured them back to his home under false pretenses. Once there, Li retracted his offer to pay them for sex and suddenly turned violent. He forced each of his victims down into his dank cellar forcibly, prodding them through the narrow tunnel until they arrived at their new home: a cold, dark, concrete room.

The following December, he used the same tactic to lure a 19-year-old named Jiang back to his property. Again, she found herself forced into the makeshift cellar.

In the spring and summer months of 2011, Li went on a spree and found three more women to trick into coming home with him: another female named Zhang (who I'll refer to as Zhang M moving forward), a 16-year-old called Cai, and another woman called Ma. Now he had a group of victims in his tiny squalid cellar. No cleaning amenities. No fresh air. No light. No water. No food. The women were desperate and in a constant state of fear, hunger, and hyperalertness.

Their captor would only feed them every few days to make sure they were in a constant state of fatigue. If his victims were weak and tired, they would be less likely to attempt to escape. Even if they did, their lack of strength would mean they'd not get very far.

Li would rape each of his captives on a regular basis. Zhang M would eventually become pregnant at the hands of her attacker.

He installed cameras and fitted a whole set-up designed to record his captives and would force the women to perform for paying customers. To defy Li's orders would mean a violent and cruel punishment. In the end, the girls learned not to say no to their abductor since he was the only one who could provide food and water. Like most criminals who hold victims against their will, Li would dangle access to food and water over their heads. He would also encourage in-fighting among the females in his dungeon and bask in the attention he was getting. Perhaps his ego wouldn't allow him to comprehend that the women were vying for his attention not because they liked him but because they wanted to survive.

If we rewind to 2010, shortly after Li abducted his first victims, Zhang and Duan, this is when Li first escalated his crimes from sexual abuse and abduction to murder. Zhang was aggressive and didn't comply with her attacker as easily as the others. This didn't sit well with Li, who would violently punish the woman for her defiance.

At some point in 2010, Zhang saw the opportunity to attack her abductor from behind. She jumped on him and began hitting her abuser, though he was stronger than her. She thought she'd caught him in a vulnerable position, but the man overpowered Zhang and beat her. Still, this didn't quell the young woman's fighting spirit, and she refused to comply with the rapist's demands. Furious, Li obtained some handcuffs and tied the woman to a bedpost. Again, this proved to do little to stop Zhang from fighting back against her attacker.

Incensed, Li decided she had to die. He enlisted the help of fellow captive Duan to aid in snuffing out the life of Zhang. He promised the woman he'd set her free if she helped him kill the problematic woman. Duan agreed, knowing what would become of her if she defied Li. The pair set about strangling Zhang as she was cuffed to the bed, taking turns throttling the woman, punching and kicking her until she took her last breath.

Li dug a hole beneath the bed and buried the body there. Duan and the rest of Li's victims would all have to live directly above the decaying corpse beneath them. The brutal murder of one of the captives was used as a cautionary tale to women who considered defying Li. Jiang, Zhang M, Cai, and Ma joined Duan in the following months, and they were all put to work making shows for customers online.

Li would instruct the women to do obscene things for the paying crowd, charging 50 yuan for 30 minutes of content. As of writing, this works out as $7 per half hour. The twisted man had compiled enough footage of the women that he was able to create over 50 videos to sell.

As you can imagine, Li spent a lot of time not just abusing the women, but also putting them to work. Recording videos, finding customers, and treating the whole sordid affair as a business took up a lot of the father-of-one's time. In an effort to conceal what he was really doing, Li told his wife he'd found extra nightshift work. On those "work" nights, he'd be in the dungeon. The sick man was not only abusing these women after stripping them of their liberty; he was making money from them. There were plenty of buyers for the content, too.

By the spring of 2011, Li discovered that Cai had developed a gynecological disease. This rendered the woman unable to carry out the obscene acts Li instructed her to do, making her worthless to the rapist. With her health problem stopping her from performing, Cai became a burden to the man; she was simply another mouth to feed when he did, in fact, feed the women.

There was only one rational solution in Li's mind: to kill Cai.

Again, he wouldn't do this alone. He enlisted the help of Duan, Jiang, Ma, and Zhang M to torture Cai to death. She was useless, he told the four of them, and to remain in his good books, they should beat the woman up.

The captives did as their captor asked, and they hit and kicked their fellow victim. While we can judge the women for this, it was a kill-or-be-killed situation, and they knew just how depraved Li was.

With Cai singled out, she was no longer receiving food or water from Li. She had to sit and watch as the other women were handed a sip of water or a small plate of food. None of the women would dare hand some of their rations to the woman - that would make them as good as dead.

What they did next was just utter cruelty, though. In a bid to please Li, the women forced Cai to drink their urine and eat their excrement. This abuse went on for weeks, with the condemned woman being beaten regularly by her fellow captives. The beatings were brutal. She was punched, kicked, stamped on, and strangled. By the end of July 2011, after one especially nasty attack, Cai's body could no longer take the abuse. Duan, in her second murder in as many years, helped Li bury the body in a hole dug beneath the dungeon.

Later that year, Li would try to earn more money from the women by selling them for sex. The man wanted to squeeze as much out of his captives as he could and make as much money from each of them as possible. But would his greed be his downfall?

By that autumn, Li had successfully coerced Duan and Zhang M into sex "work" - I use the word work here, but neither woman saw any of the money from their time exchanging their bodies for cash. In fact, they were doing it out of fear of their abuser, even though it appeared they were duly complying with Li out of respect for him. Li got comfortable letting the women visit certain hotels and return to him with cash in hand. As a result, and with his want for more money getting greater, Li forced the others out of the dungeon and into selling themselves. This would be his undoing - Ma took this opportunity to escape and fled back home.

She told her family the whole disturbing story, and they took the woman to the police station so she could make a formal complaint. What she was telling the police didn't seem believable, but once officers arrived at Li's property, they quickly found out she was telling the truth. The dungeon was where she said it would be; it looked exactly as the woman had described, and there was a victim still held hostage there: Jiang. Duan and Zhang M were at the hotel where they'd been "working" for Li. Just like Ma had said, police found the women here with paying customers.

With all four women now out of Li's line of fire, they were able to tell the police everything. Their stories corroborated one another; as unbelievable as it all sounded, there was no doubt they were telling the truth.

With all of his captives now free, Li knew the jig was up. He could either give himself up and admit his guilt or make a run for it. Li, as you can expect of such a cowardly man, chose the latter. He raced to his sister's home and asked to borrow some money so he could skip town, a request she obliged. She handed her criminal brother 1,000 yuan, and he took off out of the city. Well, almost.

Authorities captured the serial rapist before he got too far and placed him under arrest. His sister, for her part in aiding her brother to evade the law, was also arrested.

There was no denying Li's guilt. The evidence against him - and there was an abundance of it - was too great to deny. Toward the end of 2012, Li was handed the death penalty and fined 10,000 yuan.

Law enforcement wasn't just interested in Li facing justice - they also wanted to make sure the women he'd abducted faced punishment for their part in the murders of Zhang and Cai. Whether or not this was right is up for debate. The women most certainly did partake in the murders, but it was under extreme coercion and fear. They weren't willing accomplices but rather victims. Still, there was no way around the fact that the women were killers, too, and they were also put on trial.

Jiang and Zhang M got probation for their role in Cai's death. Duan, who had participated in both Cai and Zhang's murder, got a harsher sentence: three years in jail. Again, the decision to charge the women was a controversial one since it had been suggested that the women were suffering from Stockholm Syndrome and had no autonomy. But, murder is murder, some argued, and the sentences the women were given were lenient considering the crime they were accused of.

Li was executed on January 21, 2014.

Murder, He Wrote

Someone can be pure evil but still possess good qualities and have admirable skills.

Being brilliant at something doesn't automatically make you a good person, although society doesn't always seem to be able to comprehend that. We idolize celebrities and sports stars, and even when they're exposed for doing bad deeds, they can often get a free pass for their poor behavior because they have praiseworthy skills.

Jack Unterweger's case shows how fickle opinions toward an evil person can be when they exhibit an admirable talent.

He was born August 16, 1950, in Styria, Austria, to Theresia Unterweger. His father, Jack Sr, was an American soldier with whom she had a quick romance. There have been some suggestions that Theresia was a sex worker who got pregnant after an encounter with a client, though this has never been proven. Despite being with child, Theresia continued her dangerous lifestyle, which included illegal activities such as fraud. Even when she was caught for her wrongdoings, police officers could see the woman was heavily pregnant. Because of this, they were lenient with her and often let her go with little more than a caution.

However, once Jack was born, the woman found it wasn't as easy to wriggle out of the way of justice. When little Jack was just three years old, his mother was yet again arrested, and law enforcement was sick of the persistent criminal darkening their doorstep. With a jail sentence imminent for the young mother, Jack was sent to Austria to be taken care of by his grandfather. However, the boy's caregiver wasn't the affectionate, loving type, and any love offered to the child was tough, to say the least.

As Jack grew up, his grandfather taught him how to steal, and the pair would engage in illegal activities together. The caregiver, who was abusive and violent towards his grandson, would use the boy to thieve farm animals. Naturally, Jack found himself in trouble with the law from a very young age and even did some stints behind bars for his petty crimes.

By the time Jack was 16, he had decided to try to make money the honest way. He gained employment as a waiter but quickly realized that making money illegally was faster and easier. It didn't matter if people got hurt or chaos ensued: breaking the law was Jack's preferred way of living. As well as getting arrested for stealing, the teenager was also apprehended for sexually abusing a sex worker. He was also caught selling women for sex. By the time Jack was 24, he'd spent almost half his life in and out of youth-offending establishments and jail.

Jack had been harboring violent thoughts toward women for some time. Whether it was due to feeling abandoned by his mother or resentment towards his mother being labeled a sex worker, nobody truly knows the root of his disdain for women. Regardless, his searing hatred would come to a horrid climax in 1974 when he carried out his first murder.

Margaret Schäfer was an 18-year-old whom Jack propositioned for sex. When the German national refused the man's advances, he pulled out an iron bar and began beating the young woman until her face was crimson red. Then, he removed her clothing, including her bra, and wrapped the undergarment around her neck. Jack pulled the bra as tightly as he would until the woman died.

Murder by bra strap would go on to become Jack's MO.

He left Margaret's naked body in the woods, but the man left enough clues for police to tie the brutal murder back to him. At the murder trial, Jack claimed he attacked the woman because she reminded him of his mother. Perhaps he felt this defense would provoke sympathy from the jury, but it didn't. Jack was handed a life sentence for the murder in 1976.

While in jail, something peculiar happened. Jack had never been taught to read or write. He'd been brought up to lie, cheat, and steal for what he wanted. There was no need for literacy on the path he was headed down. But, while in prison, Jack learned to read and write and found a passion for putting pen to paper.

The once-illiterate man wrote prolifically and spent almost all of his waking hours consuming books or writing his own stories. He penned plays, novels, and poems. Prison guards would marvel at the criminals' beautifully crafted words and how they seamlessly flowed from chapter to chapter. Jack even spent much time writing his autobiography, translated as "Purgatory."

His work soon caused the ears of Austria's creative elite to prick up. Talk show host Peter Huemer spoke of how emotive Jack's autobiography was, noting how it made him cry. Fellow authors also praised the criminal's work. Author Elfriede Jelinek described Jack's writing as "quality," and word spread of the imprisoned man with unbelievable literary talent.

By 1985, a campaign was doing the rounds to release Jack from prison, propelled by journalists, artists, writers, and even certain politicians. The drive to pardon the murderer eventually found its way to the Austrian President, who wouldn't entertain the idea of an early release.

It seems members of the creative world couldn't compute that although Jack Unterweger had fantastic talent, he was also a violent murderer. They felt his writing ability should earn him a pardon for a sick murder. Good and bad can coexist within a person, but the good cannot rub out the evil deeds a person carries out. Think of Hitler - he did unimaginably atrocious things. Unforgivable, sickening things. But he also adored animals and established laws protecting domestic animals and wildlife. People can be evil while having commendable qualities. It doesn't dampen the malice within them.

In the spring of 1990, Jack was released from prison after serving the minimum sentence of 15 years. He was declared reformed after years of being a model prisoner. Many people celebrated his release within the creative industry, and his autobiography was used in literature lessons in Austrian schools. Job offers flooded in for the murderer, and Jack went on to host radio shows, took on journalism work, and conducted multiple interviews.

Jack was viewed as a symbol of hope for reform. That intellect would help you rise above your problems. Sadly, Jack's problem was an innate hatred towards women, and no amount of quality literature could change that. People were inclined to believe the killer had changed, though. He hadn't.

Even his own writing exposed him as misogynistic and hateful toward females. In one of his poems, he declared there was nothing more poetic than "the death of a beautiful woman."

Four months after Jack's release, Blanka Bockova, a young Czech woman, was found dead, having been strangled to death with her bra strap. Law enforcement had only come across such a bizarre method of murder once before - when they found the body of Margaret Schäfer. But it was inconceivable that Jack Unterweger was capable of carrying out this murder despite it being a direct replica of the one he was convicted of.

The months rolled by, and more young women were turning up dead. They'd all been strangled to death by their bra straps. Brunhilde Masser, Heidi Hammerer, Elfriede Schrempf, Silvia Zagler, Sabine Moitzl, Karin Eroglu-Sladky, and Regina Prem were all found beaten with their undergarments wrapped around their necks. Still, Jack wasn't hauled back in for murder. After all, he was reformed. More than this, he was a literary genius - surely he wouldn't be capable of such atrocities?

By the early 90s, Jack was making the most of his writing opportunities. He was often hired to write about crimes and sex work, topics he was clearly familiar with, although nobody saw the macabre irony. In fact, Jack would often be invited on law enforcement drives to the red light district, where they'd investigate crimes and seek his opinion on the perpetrators. One such set of crimes Jack was asked to help investigate were the murders of sex workers Irene Rodriguez, Peggy Booth, and Shannon Exley. The crimes had occurred in LA, inexplicably during the same period of time Jack had been there. Each of the women had been horrifically beaten and raped before being garroted by their bra straps.

The bodies were piling up, each of them with a bra tied around their neck. Each was sexually assaulted. Each was beaten mercilessly before their grizzly end. It was only a matter of time before Jack became a suspect. It seemed to take more than a few murders for investigators to put the pieces of the puzzle together, and by the time they had, Jack Unterweger had fled. He knew law enforcement was on to him.

An international manhunt ensued, with Jack and his girlfriend Bianca fleeing through Europe, eventually finding themselves in Miami. All the while, the criminal on the run was making contact with the Austrian media in a bid to enlist their help in getting him off the hook. He'd fooled the Austrian public once before, and Jack hoped he could get the media to do his dirty work again. It didn't seem as though he'd be lucky this time round. In February 1992, he was arrested in Florida. He was detained in Miami until his extradition back to Austria that summer.

Jack was facing 11 charges of murder but was only found guilty of nine. As part of the trial process, Jack was examined by a psychiatrist, who determined the man had NPD, narcissistic personality disorder. However, this did little to quell the jury's decision that he was a serial killer. He was handed life in jail without the possibility of parole on June 29, 1994.

That night, as he sat in his cold cell alone, Jack realized he'd used up all of his options. The artistic world could no longer propel the idea that he was a reformed man. His writing work was no longer as intriguing to the public. He was going to spend his life in jail with nothing but his pen and paper for company. He pulled the cord from the waistband of his tracksuit and de-laced his sneakers. Jack fashioned a noose and tied it around his neck. He garroted himself in the exact same way he executed all his victims. One politician would later say this was the "best murder" Jack had carried out.

Justice was never able to be served in its entirety for Jack, but at least he will be remembered for his monstrous acts over his enchanting writing. Since his death, it's been suggested that Jack didn't write all of his own material, including his highly acclaimed autobiography.

A Six-Figure Murder

The following story has been described as "the worst crime in Scotland."

Lynda Spence was a 27-year-old financial advisor and had her own property company. The young woman was doing incredibly well for herself. She even had the whole top floor of a bank as her company office, of which she was the only employee. Still, it impressed those she did business with.

The woman lived a fast-paced lifestyle filled with champagne, plenty of schmoozing with potential business prospects, and luxury shopping trips. Lynda was described as "larger than life" by those who knew her and commented how she'd always buy you the most expensive drinks when they bumped into her at the bar. The successful woman wore high-priced jewelry and designer handbags and never cheaped out when buying clothes.

For someone so young, many admired Lynda for her business acumen and her apparent wealth.

However, all wasn't as it seemed, and Lynda had been running her businesses as a front to con people out of their money. While Lynda did earn hundreds of thousands of pounds a year, it wasn't from legitimate business activities. Instead, under the guise of being a genuine businesswoman, she would take people's money for her services and never deliver on what she promised.

In fact, in 2008, Lynda was declared bankrupt. The debt was written off after 12 months, and the woman set up trading again in 2009. Her grandmother had passed away during this time, and Lynda had been left a substantial amount of money to use in getting her new venture off the ground. However, most of the money was spent on making Lynda *look* like a legitimate businesswoman rather than being spent on actually creating a legitimate business. She had all the expensive suits, the fancy car, and the posh office space. The flash veneer helped attract investors to take notice of Lynda and feel comfortable enough to work with her. After all, they thought, she must be making good money to afford all of her luxuries.

New flats were being built on Glasgow Harbor, a prestigious urban area overlooking the river. Lynda saw this as a fantastic opportunity to help those struggling to get a mortgage due to their poor financial history. Except, it was just another scheme of hers. She convinced those interested in purchasing a flat that she'd be able to secure a mortgage deal for them for a lump sum of £3,500. Lynda would falsify bank documents for the individuals and ensure they secured one of the sought-after properties. However, Lynda never made good on her promise and took £175,000 worth of payments from hopeful individuals, only for them to never step foot inside one of the promised properties.

In early 2010, Lynda became involved with an Iranian businessman she referred to as Ben. She told people she was facilitating million-pound deals with this man and began telling people they were involved in a huge deal building properties at Stansted Airport. One of the people interested in the Airport deal was Colin Coats, an entrepreneur who had dealt with Lynda in the past. If he invested £85,000 upfront, he'd get millions in return.

This was just another one of Lynda's schemes. However, it seems she underestimated just how dangerous Colin Coats was.

Colin was born September 3, 1970, in Glasgow. His interest in computers earned him a high-paying job in tech in the 90s. He would go on to become extremely wealthy in his mid-20s. He would marry and have children, and his life was what many people can only dream of achieving. He was wealthy, had a healthy family, and a career he was passionate about. However, Colin was an angry, violent man who would lash out at his wife when things didn't go his way. In 1999, he was arrested for beating his wife.

The man then decided to get into property development, further lining his pockets. Colin would mention how everything he touched turned to gold, and for a while, that was true. He was making more money per month than many of us earn in a whole year, and he got to a point where most of his income was passive. With little to do during his days, he turned to drugs and alcohol. Addiction to substances soon followed, as did persistent violent and abusive behavior from Colin. By 2007, his wife could no longer endure her husband's fierce temper, and she filed for divorce.

As you can imagine, the hotheaded man didn't take this lightly. He'd ram his ex's car if he ever saw her out and about. On one occasion, shortly after the separation, Colin saw his wife's sister in the city and attacked her. An older man tried to intervene, but he, too, received a beating from the rage-filled man. Justice rarely caught up with Colin since any time he did something illegal like this, he'd flee the country to his second home in Spain. Still, even on the plane to Costa Blanca, a two-and-a-half-hour flight, he couldn't contain his antisocial behavior.

On a 2010 flight, he attacked passengers, threatened to attack children with acid, and to blow up the aircraft with everyone on it. Around this time, Colin had begun getting involved with organized criminals, which led him to meet a man named Philip Wade. Colin met Lynda Spence after being introduced by Philip, and he and Lynda soon began doing business together.

However, it became apparent to Colin that Lynda wasn't making good on her promises to return his investments or repay loans on time. Still, Lynda had a way of keeping people on her side and managed to convince him to invest even more money with her. This time, it was for plots of land at Stansted Airport. The idea of this investment generating him millions of pounds was enough to blind Colin to Lynda's lies, and yet again, he transferred the woman a lump sum of money.

As time passed, it became increasingly clear to Colin that he wouldn't be getting his money back, let alone a return on his investment. Yet again, Lynda had scammed him.

Colin was an egotistical man and felt his reputation in the criminal underworld he was involved with had been ruined by Lynda. He felt he wouldn't be taken seriously if people knew he'd been scammed time and time again by the woman, and he began to make plans to ensure his money was returned. He turned to his good friend Philip Wade, who sympathized with Colin's situation; it turned out that the woman had also duped Philip.

While Philip had been serving time in jail, he contacted Lynda to do him a favor. He needed to make sure his kids got Christmas presents from him, and without being able to do the shopping himself, he sent Lynda £700 to pick up some gifts for his family. The woman accepted the money but spent all the money on herself.

She'd made enemies out of Colin and Philip, and when the two discussed how they'd get revenge, a twisted plan was conceived. On April 14, 2011, the plan was carried out. The disgruntled pair lured Lynda from her house and abducted her, taking her to a quiet street in West Kilbride. They flung her inside a dilapidated flat and tied her to a chair. The property was in disarray and was unlivable due to the rubble and debris on the floor. Lynda was bound in the attic, which was even less inhabitable. Tape was tightly wound around the terrified woman's mouth, and she was unable to move from the chair she was strapped to. Her captors blindfolded their victim.

Colin stood over Lynda and dropped the toolbag in his hands. It clunked as it hit the floor, and although Lynda couldn't see what was happening, she could certainly hear the noise the tools made. In this scenario, the tools would be used as torture weapons, which included garden shears and a hot steam iron.

Colin removed the blindfold and demanded to know where his money was. Lynda didn't have an answer for Colin, so he proceeded to punch the woman in the head and face, beating her black and blue. Still, the victim couldn't offer an answer that satisfied him. He stubbed his lit cigarette out on her before taking the woman's phone. Colin and Philip messaged Lynda's family, pretending to be her so nobody would be too concerned about her whereabouts.

More beatings ensued for Lynda, and they were relentless. However, she did get a break when Colin and Philip had other things to deal with. When the two men were absent from the flat, they enlisted the help of two small-time thugs to watch over Lynda. David Parker and Paul Smith were tasked with various shifts of staying at the run-down flat and ensuring Lynda never got free from her chair. For their troubles, they'd been promised £10,000.

The woman wasn't even freed when she needed to use the bathroom. She had to go where she sat - and she sat there for 14 days in her own waste. You can only imagine the agony she was in as the days passed and her injuries were multiplying.

On day three or four, Colin brought a golf club to the attack and began a prolonged and violent attack on Lynda. He swung at her body, limbs, and face, demanding the money. He paid extra attention to the woman's kneecaps, making sure to shatter them with the club.

If Lynda had the money to give him, you'd assume she'd let him have it by this point. Nobody but Colin, Philip, and Lynda know exactly what she said when he demanded the money, but it's clear she could not obtain it for him. Still, the violent man would only escalate his barbarity.

Lynda was now swollen from head to toe. Her whole body would have been in agonizing pain, and it's likely she drifted in and out of consciousness throughout her ordeal. However, Colin wasn't done, not by a long shot.

He retrieved a hot steam iron and held it down on the brutalized woman's bare skin, burning her flesh until it fell from her body. He repeated this sick torture on various parts of Lynda's anatomy. Her mouth taped shut, she was unable to scream. Even if she did, there was nobody to hear her cries; plus, a cry for help would result in even more brutal torture from Colin Coats.

As the days passed, Colin and Philip remained in contact with Lynda's loved ones, pretending to be her. If they only knew what their loved one was enduring at the hands of two barbaric men.

The abuse would only get worse when Colin pulled out his garden shears and placed the blades over Lynda's thumb. The woman was powerless to stop the frenzied man from snapping the blades together and removing her thumb. He would repeat this violent act on one of her fingers, too, before picking up the fingers and bundling them into a plastic bag.

Pliers were brought out afterward, and each and every one of Lynda's toes was crushed with the implement.

The woman was unrecognizable at this point. She was systematically being tortured to death, and three people knew what Colin was doing yet didn't alert the police. The small-time thugs who watched over the women would make her cups of tea from time to time, but she was unable to drink unaided.

Meanwhile, Colin had also made contact with another man Lynda had scammed out of money, John Glen. He was a property developer who'd "invested" in one of Lynda's schemes but, like so many before him, hadn't seen any kind of return on his investment. By John's own admission, Lynda had been making some small efforts to repay him and had returned almost £50,000 by the time Colin Coats had got in touch with him.

However, Colin's pleasant facade soon faded, and he began to get nasty with John. He claimed the £50,000 Lynda had repaid him wasn't hers to repay - it belonged to Colin. John was naturally confused, and the confusion soon turned to horror when Colin reached inside his coat pocket to present a severed thumb to him. He advised it belonged to Lynda and threatened to kill John if he didn't pay off Lynda's debts toward him.

When Colin returned to the West Kilbride, he resumed his torture of the woman. Just over a week passed, and Colin and Philip were no closer to having their money returned to them. It seemed that as much as Lynda was good at obtaining money, she wasn't good at keeping it. She liked to spend, and any money they'd given her had now gone. When Colin and Philip arrived at the flat on the morning of April 27, the pair let David Parker and Paul Smith off their night shift. They wouldn't be needed anymore.

Colin held the woman's nose until she died. Tape remained around her mouth, meaning she had no chance of gasping for even a little air. Immediately afterward, the pair began cleaning up the blood-stained crime scene. First of all, they dismembered Lynda, chopping off her extremities and even removing her head. Then, they gave the property a thorough cleaning. The pair then bundled Lynda's limbs, torso, and head into the car and drove off to dispose of her.

By May of that year, Colin and Philip had given up texting Lynda's family. They felt no need to keep up the facade. She was eventually reported missing, and a police hunt ensued. Lynda's parents, Jim and Patricia, made pleas to the public for anybody who knew anything to come forward. Patricia took part in an emotional press release, begging her daughter to come home.

The investigation into Lynda's sudden disappearance revealed her shady business dealings, and it was suggested she may have fled abroad to avoid the repercussions from disgruntled business partners. Then, an interesting fact came to light: Lynda had been working as an undercover informer for the Scottish Crime and Drugs Enforcement Agency and was working on a case against some dangerous criminals before her disappearance. Nobody knew about Lynda's double life, but it seemed like wherever she'd gone, it was to escape the wrath of angry criminals.

However, the more the police delved into Lynda's life, the more they found one name in particular cropping up: Colin Coats. Every avenue the officers went down seemed to offer little in the way of clues, though. People who knew Colin were too afraid to speak about him, but the police were confident the man had something to do with Lynda's disappearance. They ended up putting the criminal under surveillance, watching his every move. *Surely he'd slip up somewhere*, they hoped.

Eventually, he did. Colin met up with John Glen and threatened the man again for money. This time, John went to the police and told them everything he knew, including the fact that Colin had shown him Lynda's severed thumb. Still, officers needed time to gather evidence to present a case against Colin Coats. It took them six months before they got the details of where Lynda spent her last two weeks alive. They raided the flat, and it was clear something sinister had gone on there. Despite Colin and Philip cleaning the place up, there were still drops of Lynda's blood inside the property, and the chair she'd been brutalized in was sitting in the garden.

Colin Coates, Philip Wade, David Parker, and Paul Smith were all arrested. The two small-time crooks offered to tell the police everything they knew about Lynda's murder, which added more damning evidence against Colin and Philip, who were denying having anything to do with the woman's disappearance. Philip would end up suggesting that Lynda had stayed with them willingly to escape some violent criminals, although the court didn't buy this for one moment. The pair were found guilty of murder. Colin got a minimum of 33 years, while Philip got 30 years.

For years, neither man would admit their guilt, much less tell anyone where the woman's body was. Lynda's mother pleaded with the men to tell her where her daughter's body was, but they remained tightlipped - until 2022. In a huge turnaround, Colin Coats seemingly admitted his guilt and guided the police to a field where he said Lynda was. Patricia Spence even began arranging a funeral for her daughter, but the search of the area didn't turn up any remains. "Give me Lynda back before anything happens to me," Patrica begged her child's killers.

It's unclear if Colin legitimately thought he was giving the police the right location to dig up Lynda's remains or if he was toying with the Spence family. When you consider the evil this man is capable of, the latter doesn't seem too far-fetched.

Patricia, 57, and Jim, 69, live in the hope that they'll be able to lay their daughter to rest in their lifetime. Their hopes are pinned on Colin Coats finally doing the right thing. We can only hope he eventually does, and the Spence family can finally have some small sliver of closure.

Final Thoughts

Thank you for reading *Unbelievable Crimes Volume Seven.*

At the end of every volume, and despite this being number seven, I take a look back at the cases covered, and I'm always dismayed at the depravity some people are capable of. The fact that evil rapists, child killers, and torturous thugs exist is enough to make you question just about everything in life. The more you sit and ponder why such evil exists, how it can prevail in the world, and how so many criminals are never brought to justice, it's enough to give you anxiety. The unfairness, the unjustness, and the unbalancedness of it all can be too much to contemplate.

When I feel this way, I have to remember that there is good in the world, and generally, people are good. I do my best to add kindness and compassion to everything I do, and everywhere I go. Although if confronted with some of the evil I've detailed in this book, I'm not sure those traits would remain.

True crime can be a heavy subject to digest. Some cases affect you more than others, and some can be so disturbing that you avoid reading any true crime for a period of time. However, it can also help you stay vigilant, alert, and knowledgeable on what to look out for when someone may not be as harmless as they seem.

The topic of true crime can often get a bad rap as a dark, twisted subject that breeds hypervigilance and paranoia. For those of us who take an interest in the topic, we know different. Not only can consuming true crime remind us just how fragile life is, but it also helps us honor those who lost their lives at the hands of monsters.

It engenders our innate compassion and empathy. It allows us to be exposed to the dark side of life without our own being at risk. It makes us ask ourselves difficult questions and confront equally tricky answers. Some cases show us just how resilient we are. Others show us just how delicate we are when we find ourselves in the wrong place at the wrong time.

It reminds me of my dad's favorite saying: *always expect the unexpected.*

Once again, thank you for reading this installment of Unbelievable Crimes. I truly appreciate you taking the time to read my books. I didn't expect to have the readership I do when I first began writing, and I've been blown away by the interest these books have gotten. As a true crime follower, first and foremost, I'm glad to be able to cover crimes that perhaps never got the coverage they ought to have when they happened.

If you find the time to leave a review, I'd be extremely grateful. It helps get the book out to a wider audience, in turn allowing me to continue writing!

Until next time,

Daniela

My upcoming newsletter sign-up link: danielaairlie.carrd.co[1]

---

1. http://danielaairlie.carrd.co

Also by Daniela Airlie

Infamous Crimes
Infamous Cults: The Life and Crimes of Cult Leaders and Their Followers

Unbelievable Crimes
Unbelievable Crimes Volume One: Macabre Yet Unknown True Crime Stories
Unbelievable Crimes Volume Two: Macabre Yet Unknown True Crime Stories
Unbelievable Crimes Volume Three: Macabre Yet Unknown True Crime Stories
Unbelievable Crimes Volume Four: Macabre Yet Unknown True Crime Stories
Unbelievable Crimes Volume Five: Macabre Yet Unknown True Crime Stories
Unbelievable Crimes Volume Six: Macabre Yet Unknown True Crime Stories
Unbelievable Crimes Volume Seven
Unbelievable Crimes Volume Eight

Unbelievable Crimes Volume Nine: Macabre Yet Unknown True Crime Stories

www.ingramcontent.com/pod-product-compliance
Lightning Source LLC
Chambersburg PA
CBHW052101110526
44591CB00013B/2301